Advancing Technological Civilisation
and the threats to its existence

Robert Corfe is not only a prolific writer on political and socio-economic topics, but is experienced in party political life both locally and on the national level. His successful journalistic career dates from the 1960s, and through extensive study, he has acquired considerable knowledge of the social sciences, history and philosophy. After a long business career in senior management in a manufacturing environment, promoting home-based productivity, and later as a management consultant, he founded the Campaign for Industry in 1987 to confront the damaging tendencies of international finance. Lord Gregson of Stockport was elected President of the association, and for over a decade Corfe wrote many pamphlets on the problems of industry and the question of more widely distributing the assets of wealth. His ten years in Scandinavia, in addition to business travels throughout the world, have given him a broad perspective of the needs of all humanity.

By the same author –

The Crisis of Democracy
in the advanced industrial economies

Social Capitalism in theory and practice
Vol. I
Emergence of the New Majority
Vol. II
The People's Capitalism
Vol. III
Prosperity in a stable World

Egalitarianism of the Free Society
and the end of class conflict

The Future of Politics
with the demise of the left/right confrontational system

The Democratic Imperative
the reality of power relationships in the Nation State

Deism and Social Ethics
The role of religion in the third millennium

The Death of Socialism
the irrelevance of the traditional left & the call for a progressive Politics of universal humanity

Populism Against Progress
and the collapse of aspirational values

Freedom from America
for safeguarding democracy & the economic & cultural integrity of peoples

Land of the Olympians
papers from the enlightened Far North

This Was My England
the story of a Childhood

Advancing Technological Civilisation

and the threats to its existence

Robert Corfe

Arena Books

Copyright © Robert Corfe 2021

The right of Robert Corfe to be identified as author of this work has been asserted in accordance with the Copyright, Designs and Patents Act 1988.

First published by Arena Books in 2021

Arena Books
6 Southgate Green
Bury St. Edmunds
IP33 2BL.

www.arenabooks.co.uk

All rights reserved. Except for the quotation of short passages for the purposes of criticism and review, no part of this publication may be reproduced, stored in a retrieval system, or transmitted, in any form or by any means, electronic, mechanical, photocopying, recording or otherwise, without the prior permission of the publisher.

Corfe, Robert- 1935
Advancing Technological Civilisation and the threats to its existence

British Library cataloguing in Publication Data. A Catalogue record for this book is available from the British Library.

ISBN 978-1-911593-82-9

BIC categories:- KCA, KCP, KCX, KNB, HBG, JFCX, JFCA, JFFC, JFFD, JFFL, JFFN, JFFP, JFMD, JHBA.

Printed & bound by Lightning Source UK

Cover design
by Jason Anscomb

Typeset in
Times New Roman

DEDICATED

To the example of the Finnish people
amongst the best governed in
the world
&
To the many friends I made in that country whilst living and working there throughout the 1960s as a teacher and journalist contributing to a broad section of the Finnish press.

PREFACE

"The true test of civilisation is not the census, not the size of cities, not the crops, - no, but the kind of man the country turns out."

Ralph Waldo Emerson, *Society and Solitude: Civilisation*

In this age of uncertainty, there is the need for ideas that transcend the limitations of party political, or left/right thinking, in resolving the unprecedented problems of our time. Technological Civilisation is here presented as a focal point for a fresh perspective of both national and international issues.

The tension between America and China indicates the possibility of a new Cold War, and this would be a disaster for the planet in diverting attention away from other urgent problems, most notably the cooperation needed in attending to climate change and other threats to the environment. Whilst on the one hand, concern may be felt over China's naval manoeuvres in the Pacific around the Philippines; on the other hand, America's blame on China for her poor economic performance, is entirely self-inflicted as we shall clearly demonstrate.

On turning to the internal problems of the West, democracy as we know it is beginning to disintegrate. This is made evident through the collapse of voting figures and party memberships, as well as a spirit of disillusion. The cause is the transformation of society and the world of work over the past 60 years. The success of the left/right struggle as a democratic methodology for advancing progress over the past 200 years, has now outlived its purpose. It is now proving counter-productive, both as a form of government and as a guide to life in society. The irony is that 60 years of democratic legislation in increasing living standards, better education, and freedom for the majority, was accountable to the beneficent process of the left/right conflict which has now been turned against itself.

This has occurred through the emergence of a new middle majority, absorbing those from both the apex and lower levels of society. The old Working and Middle classes, together with their separate values, are fast disappearing, together with the ideological beliefs that polarised political life between left and right. The new middle majority is still a mixed or heterogeneous class, but the more socially aware or thinking people in its midst are appalled by politicians' call to divisiveness when the genuine grounds for such are no longer there. Existing politics therefore points to regression rather than progress. The fact is that the new social unity has destroyed the proportional structure of society in making possible a desirable dual-party system. Constructive policies for the regeneration of democracy are considered towards the end of the book.

The following book therefore examines the socio-economic undercurrents of political life that rarely appear as discussion topics in the conflicts of the party political world. This is because the superficiality of surface issues tend to conceal the underlying causes of events that attract the attention and interest of the majority – or certainly the ordinary voter.

There are some topics which politicians across the political spectrum are loathed to address, and in the sphere of the approaching environmental crisis, the population explosion is the most prominent. Many leading scientists have already demonstrated that even if all efforts are made towards reversing climate change through maximising the uses of wind-power, solar panels, and other renewable sources, etc., unless both population control and reduction is achieved on a sufficient level, all will be in vain.

No scientists have, as yet, produced a satisfactory answer to the population question, but it is a priority issue that is taken up for serious discussion in this book. In concentrating, on what may be described, as the helpful neutral values of Technological Civilisation, it is possible to discern the interconnection of problems, and this leads to constructive proposals for the regeneration of democracy, the reform of the financial-industrial system, and the emergence of an upwardly mobile and free egalitarian society.

A broad canvas is covered in arguing for the necessity of new and constructive thinking if progress is to be made. There is a long section on the barriers to free thought at the present time. This includes a critique of the trap in which higher education is caught; the damage that postmodernism has inflicted on intellectual life worldwide; and the debasing values of the entertainment industry, particularly broadcasting, which has increasingly dropped its standards over the past five decades.

It is believed that much of this has resulted through the work of hidden powerful forces, operating along the age-old principle of "bread and circuses" to keep the public quiet. Political censorship is either the cause of the above factors or the result of them. The author has long been of the opinion that those in the West who talk about "censorship" must to some degree be victims of paranoia, or "fantasising," but he cites an example of political censorship in contemporary Britain that is likely to unfailingly shock any reader of this book. This censorship is not concerned with restricting the freedom of an individual, or minor association, but a major financial publication with a worldwide reputation for accuracy and good judgement. All this goes to show there is something awry with our society, and the ruling establishment that is ultimately responsible.

The advance of Technological Civilisation cannot become a practical reality without an effective organisation to promote the cause. The latter must be presented as a credible leadership body that may persuade the rest of the planet to willingly follow. With this in mind, it is proposed that the advanced industrial economies form a Tripartite Alliance of three geographical blocs, comprising Europe; North America (to include Canada) with the addition of Australia and New Zealand; and the Confucian economies of China, Korea, Japan, Taiwan, and Singapore. The three blocs comprise many varied peoples and cultures, and their political systems emphasise these differences. The latter may only be overcome, firstly, through their educational and industrial advantage, and the feeling of unity that may be drawn from this; and secondly, through a set of enlightenment values that transcend national interests, in promoting the idea of Technological civilisation. Much of the book is devoted to discussing these issues.

The advance of Technological Civilisation offers a huge opportunity for the creation of new knowledge in the sphere of socio-economic and political ideas; and the riddance of bankrupt and out-dated thinking. Not only may the achievement of such civilisation offer renewal to all nation states, but on the international scale, to long-lasting peace and stability for our planet.

Once again, I have endeavoured to produce an index that offers an easy guide or reminder of the many topics discussed, together with additional information, as useful dates and clarification of the names of associations where only abbreviations are made in the main text.

CONTENTS

Preface - 9

Chapter 1
The many Facets of Technological Civilisation - 15
Chapter 2
The Consequences of Over-population - 29
Chapter 3
The Road to Progress - 35
Chapter 4
The Vulnerability of Civilisations - 43
Chapter 5
The Fatal Flaw of the Financial System - 50
Chapter 6
The Threat to Western Democracy - 59
Chapter 7
The Barriers to Free Thinking - 69
Chapter 8
Political Censorship in Contemporary Britain - 85
Chapter 9
The Environmental Threat to Planet Earth - 96
Chapter 10
New Approaches to the Population Problem - 103

Appendix - 123
Guide to Further Reading - 129
Index - 147

CHAPTER 1
The Many Facets of Technological Civilisation

"All our environmental problems become easier to solve with fewer people, and harder – and ultimately impossible - to solve with ever more people."

Sir David Attenborough, *Population Maters* website

The existence of Technological Civilisation is the most important factor in the world today, not only because it has raised the material standards of humankind to the highest level ever known, but because we are so deeply indebted for the intellectual potential and freedom it has granted, in addition to the incidental benefits of the arts and sciences in every conceivable field.

It should therefore be the primary object of study by those committed to resolving major political questions, for the reason that sufficient knowledge and understanding may be extracted from the topic in properly addressing all connecting socio-economic and other inter-disciplinary issues. In other words, no other starting point for the study of improving humankind or the environment on which he is dependent, or in warding off ills that might harm his future, would be sufficiently broad in including the various conflicting factors to be necessarily considered.

If party political, national, or other group interests of any kind, were taken as the starting point for such a discussion, such problems would quickly be compounded and confused rather than resolved. The same would apply to an even greater degree in the event of citing such abstract or other well-intentioned motives as the starting point for such discussion. The concept of Technological Civilisation has infinite breadth, but it also has an uncompromising neutrality in regard to purpose. This is partly due to the fact it extends beyond the interests of humankind, to include the environment of the planet and beyond. If poor decision-making is made in its name, then that is regression, and so contradicts the true purpose of Technological Civilisation when it may only be defined as progress.

If many of the major ills in the world today are directly accountable to its existence, such as poverty or famine in developing territories, or over-population, then their resolution can only be found through Technological Civilisation, for only that is technically capable of addressing such issues. If over-population is seen as the greatest threat of our time in undermining every aspect of the planet's ecosystem, then this is in great part due to advances in medical science in promoting good health and extending lifespan. These are the positive benefits of Technological Civilisation, but their incidental or adverse consequences are not to be resolved through repudiating such civilisation, or by "turning back the clock."

Civilisation can and should only move forward through experience and experimentation, correcting errors as they occur, towards ever-developing progress. This is because there is no other reasonable or practicable path to take. There will always be opposition to the concept of Technological Civilisation as progress by those minorities trapped in cultures of ancient ways who feel the burden of oppression. Where injustice is found, it should be removed, but the proponents of Technological Civilisation should never doubt its purpose, and are best united in furthering its advance.

But technological progress cannot be taken for granted. It is not inevitable as an everlasting process. As with all civilisations, as observed over the past few thousand years, Technological Civilisation is also confronted by its own set of threats. These are internal as well as external, and the greatest immediate threats are those that are internal.

The survival of any civilisation is most dependent on the Will for its existence, or self-assurance in its value and moral worth. As soon as self-doubt creeps in, then its foundations are shaken to the core. Surprisingly, civilisations, as with nation states, do not initially arise through the windfall of wealth, or valued natural resources, but often through inexplicable will-power alone – although wealth of one kind or another, soon becomes a stepping stone to expansion.

Rome, for example, sprang from an insignificant town amongst threatening and powerful neighbours. In modern times, two insignificant islands, on either side of a great landmass rose suddenly to power: Britain at the end of the 16th century, and Japan at the end of the 19th. Whilst Britain was almost annihilated by Spain, Japan was threatened by US gun-boat diplomacy. Whilst in the centuries that followed, Britain built the largest of world empires; in 1905, Japan, a land almost deprived of natural resources, had meanwhile defeated the world's largest territorial power and sent their Pacific fleet to the bottom of the ocean. Such dramatic expectations from either could never have been anticipated.

It may be interesting to note that towards the end of the 15th century, when approaches were made to finance Christopher Columbus's voyage in search of a shorter route to India, Henry VII responded by explaining that England was "a poor country with no such intention of embarking on foreign adventures." It should not be assumed his response was entirely influenced by a mean-spirited attitude to expenditure, for the Wars of the Roses had ended less than a decade earlier, and this destructive conflict amongst the nobility, had left the country greatly weakened.

When irritation arose between Russia and Japan over the Korean frontier, the Emperor of Germany urged his Russian cousin, the Tsar, to rehabilitate his politically diminished reputation by, "teaching those yellow monkeys a lesson." The outcome was the humiliation of Russia on both land and sea followed by the first Revolution of 1905. Whilst the will to power may lead to the success of an otherwise un-endowed nation state, the comforts of superfluous wealth, as we shall note in a later chapter of this book, may on the contrary lead to precipitous decline.

In returning to the Technological Civilisation of the present time, its potential power base may initially be identified through the status of the three territorial blocs of Europe, North America (including Canada) with the addition of Australia and New Zealand, and the Confucian cultures of China, Korea, Japan, Taiwan and Singapore. Despite the cultural or socio-political separateness between these three blocs, they are nonetheless fated by history – irrespective of whether or not they are prepared to accept it – as a moral imperative.

If Technological Civilisation is to survive, this may only be through such leadership over the planet. The prime purpose of what may be described as a prospective Tripartite Alliance would be to ensure the survival of our planet against climate change and other threats to the environment. The fulfilment of such a function is essential, as the alternative possibility of equal representation amongst all nation states, could never hope to achieve the political consensus required. And consensus amongst such a Tripartite Alliance can only emerge through the mutuality of their power together with the materialism of their rationality. The Alliance would perhaps best be directed or coordinated from the Netherlands as probably the country most acceptable to all those involved.

Russia's temporary inability for inclusion in such a Tripartite arrangement would be accountable to the tragedy of her present instability and uncertain relationship with the West. The chaos following the break-up of the Soviet Union after the events of 1989 must be appreciated. Greedy Western bankers attempted to take advantage for their own benefit, and compounded an already complex situation, whilst Western politicians stood indecisively aside, unable or unwilling to assist.

After ten years of appalling social conditions, as the country emerged from the failed Communist leadership, the population awoke to realise they had somehow lost vast areas of their former territory. This must have given rise to resentment and major trauma. A comparison might be made if Britain had suddenly lost Cornwall, Wales, Scotland, Northern Ireland, and her Eastern counties from Middlesbrough down to Kent. Is it, therefore, any wonder that a spirit of frustration in the hope of recovering a small part of the territory lost was a natural outcome of such humiliation?

It is hoped that Russia eventually returns to a state of stable normality, with firm government granting freedom and prosperity and the rule of law to her people, when she may then be welcomed to re-join Europe as a first nation Technological power. A not dissimilar question might also be raised as to Britain's exact status in such a European bloc in view of her Brexit decision and the crisis to which it is leading.

Those who have read my earlier books may have noted criticism of the EU, but I have never advocated departure from the Union. We entered in rushed and difficult circumstances in the early 1970s, when no proper negotiations had been made for necessary special conditions as had been allowed our neighbours. Either our civil servants had been wimps in negotiating, or just negligent in attending to our interests. At the time, I was deeply involved in freight forwarding and the technicalities surrounding duties and levies, and plainly anticipated trouble in an unknown future.

It would have been better had we remained within the EU, but raised a voice of protest – even to the level of threats – but preferably to regain our rightful status for the greater benefit of all. If we measure the level of our current trade with the EU by a realistic comparison with the potentially limited level of trade with the rest of the world, our departure from the market is little short of madness since it is dependent on imaginary estimates with little basis in fact.

In their role as advanced technological cultures, the countries of the proposed Tripartite Alliance should be held as of equal status irrespective of population or geographical size. Hence Estonia or Denmark should be held in equal regard and share an equal voice with that of America or China. The size of a country is no indication of the quality of government, and the dedication of this book is a recognition of that fact. Only through such an arrangement would trust and true cooperation be viable.

This is not to suggest that the front runners of our Technological Civilisation are similar in their approach to political reality or interpretation as to the best path for progress; but it does imply their equality in terms of potential technological development and understanding. All nations have their separate traditions and style of expression, and these should be respected. In the West, we have always spoken about *Western Civilisation*, but in prioritising its technological aspect, this is a term that should no longer be correctly applied on a global basis. Hence, in including the countries of the Far East, it is more meaningful to refer to our shared *Technological Civilisation*.

ADVANCING TECHNOLOGICAL CIVILISATION 21

The need for using this term is emphasised by the fact that the Confucian cultures may outpace the West in the not too distant future. The fact that both America and Britain, and to a lesser extent, several other European countries have in great part forsaken the home-based manufacture of tangibles in exchange for a usurious financial system based on investment in passive assets and overseas interests, morally justifies the competitive edge of the Far East. The polarisation of wealth in Britain and America into the hands of the super-rich, whilst limiting the power of the newly emerging middle majority, is already undermining democracy. A sound social purpose in benefiting the majority should underpin the leadership of a proposed Tripartite Alliance, as otherwise it would lose its moral credibility with the world beyond. This is a theme to which we shall return in greater detail in a later chapter.

The greatest reservation of the West in regard to the Confucian cultures – or at least, in Regard to China and to a lesser extent to Singapore – is their interpretation and practice of democracy. The argument of this book is that their limited interpretations of democratic government would be insufficient in carrying their peoples forward for the indefinite future. The counter response of both China and Singapore to such a suggestion is that they could not possibly have raised the living and educational standards of their peoples to such a high level, within so short a time-period had they waited patiently for democracy to fully evolve. There is no answer to the truth of such a contention.

Nonetheless, the Chinese interpretation is wanting in fulfilling the more distant needs of the future. This is because, as maintained in this book – as I have always argued - that complete freedom of thought, expression and action within peaceful limits is vital in enabling progress on a permanent or never-ending basis. Progress of a kind is always possible under any form of government, but unless full freedom in practice is upheld in society, there always reaches a point when progress will suddenly cease for an inexplicable reason. This is sometimes due to the complacency of the state in announcing that the perfection of society and knowledge can no longer be improved upon; or that change is suddenly decided to be undesirable for the greater good, and restrictive legislation follows in its wake.

It may be noted in this context that China has already been stopped in its tracks on at least one occasion. Around the year 1500, both China and Western Europe were technologically on an equal par. In some ways, China was in advance of Europe: for example, she was building ocean going ships twenty times the size of Christopher Columbus's *Santa Maria*, and her manufacture of chinaware was far in advance of anything then produced in the West, and printing and widespread literacy in that country preceded that in Europe.

At a time when both civilisations were hardly aware of the other, the Chinese authorities under the Ming dynasty, reduced the navy, forbad further overseas exploration, having already traded with India, the Arabian peninsula and along the coast of East Africa, and then announced that the "Middle Kingdom" was self-sufficient for all her worldly needs. In this way began the long period of self-isolation and decline into a state of satisfied senescence.

Meanwhile, Western Europe shot ahead technologically at a faster pace than any civilisation had experienced in history. The reason stemmed not from the grant of "freedom" in a pre-democratic age, but from the consequences of intensive competition and warfare amongst a dozen or so leading nation states sharing an approximate equality of material development. This struggle amongst equals maintained a constant stimulus towards technological growth, culminating in breaking beyond their landmass and establishing imperial territories throughout the globe. The moral justification for territorial expansion was naturally the argument for trade, or the mutual exchange of goods, together with the benefits of a higher civilisation. The additional argument of imposing a new religion (or religious mindset) on distant peoples is something we can no longer concur with, but the later emergence of democracy as an apt system of government for all humankind was wholly beneficial in its intended purpose.

If the above suggests a possible reservation on China and Singapore on the grounds of their interpretation of democracy, here in the West, as noted above, we have no reason for complacency in regard to our own democracy as we find it today. In the Western world, democracy as we have known it is beginning to disintegrate, especially in the dual-party confrontational systems of America and Britain. This is a consequence of the transformation of society and the world of work over the past 60 years, and the collapse of the left/right conflict as an apt medium in advancing progress. A new and more effective mode of democracy will be needed to replace that which is discredited and in process of self-desolation. Again, this is a subject to which we shall return in a later chapter.

It may therefore be appreciated that all three blocs comprising a proposed Tripartite Alliance have differing socio-economic systems that clearly set them apart. Europe, with her social democratic and welfare systems is hardly less divided in her socio-economic thinking from America than she is from China. The American mindset with its aggressive individualism, giving rise to its particular type of social sickness, disdains the idea of "welfare" as trampling on freedom; and views European society as half-way between irresponsible indolence and pseudo-communism. Whilst such differences between the three blocs should be mutually tolerated and respected as long as they last, the underlying factor of their technological advance and the higher educational status of their majorities, should nonetheless stand as an overriding influence in enabling their eventual unity with a new purpose in mind.

As with any agreement amongst advanced industrial nations, the proposed Tripartite Alliance comprising our Technological Civilisation, as defined above, should be committed to social justice in the cause of upward mobility of all peoples to eventual equality. This should be linked to an authority based on factual knowledge and skills in the resolution of socio-economic and other issues affecting nation states, e.g., border disputes, the right to controlling waterways, or natural disasters, etc.

The countries comprising our Technological Civilisation should not only seek to work in the closest cooperation and harmony amongst themselves, but avoid any step that might possibly lead to a conflict situation. This is because recent history has demonstrated that when peace is maintained amongst front line states, then world peace is assured, whilst if this is broken, then the most destructive conflicts often result in inflicting suffering on all involved.

As all nation states differ according to cultural, language, and geographical factors, and access to natural resources, all nations have differing needs. For this reason, every nation should put its own interests first, especially in regard to self-sustainability and resisting the power of international finance that too often exploits one sector of the population against another, or uses its power for tax evasion through offshore centres, or otherwise defrauds the majority population. Over recent years, the call of globalisation has lost its lure with both left and right for differing reasons. National interests should be upheld through an international nationalism of common understanding and appreciation for the needs of all.

The most urgent and primary reason for calling into being a Tripartite Alliance for world leadership under the heading of Technological Civilisation is to confront the oncoming catastrophe to the environment through climate change, and rising temperatures, that may certainly destroy within several centuries all animal life. This is not merely a threat but a certainty if no counter measures are taken.

Although "climate change" and "environment" maybe on everyone's lips during these disturbing times, the single overwhelming cause of the problem is rarely mentioned. Global afforestation; the restoration of the rain forest; the building of windfarms; the utilisation of tidal power; the widespread development of desalination plants; the far greater use of solar panels in generating power; the elimination of single-use non-recyclable plastics; and the withdrawal from use of harmful pesticides and fertilisers that damage the long-term value of the soil or poison water resources, etc., are all necessary measures, but even if carried to their furthest extent, they will hardly touch on the greater underlying problem. And that underlying problem is over-population, an issue that all politicians across the political spectrum are loathed to mention – let alone, to discuss.

The reason for this reticence – regrettable as it is bearing in mind the level of threats – is easy to comprehend. The discussion of over-population – and even more so, the call for its reduction – is not a topic to attract the happy intentions of the ordinary politician. The party politician operates within narrow self-interested motives, with future votes always in mind. This calls for an optimistic rather than pessimistic view of existence. It is difficult to discuss the topic of over-population, or the need for an aspect of human restraint that conflicts with the species survival, without projecting a disagreeable view of humankind. Politicians are far too savvy in protecting their popularity to raise controversial issues so personally close to their electorates.

The threats of over-population are therefore best left to scientists such as David Attenborough, or James Lovelock, or such thinkers as Paul R. Ehrlich, Sara Parkin, Sir Crispin Tickell, or Malcolm Potts, working at a distance from electoral politics, and so free to take a more disinterested approach to urgent issues. Until the relatively recent past, the Malthusian arguments on population growth were often rejected on the promise of agricultural improvements in increasing the food supply. It is true that the later and enlarged editions of, *An Essay on the Principle of Population*, appeared in the post-Napoleonic era of poverty and mass unemployment, and that huge advances in agriculture were made in the following 200 years. But today we find these advances have not only entailed the poisoning of the soil and water sources through chemical fertilisers and pesticides, but that populations are exceeding the extent to meet necessary food supplies by any means.

The adverse consequences of over-population are inescapable, and must therefore be confronted with the openness that honesty demands. There is no longer room to hide behind the mask of "magicking" into existence an ever-increasing food supply; or the hope that "moral restraint," to use the curious phrase of Thomas Malthus, will somehow resolve the situation. Every country will face the crisis in slightly differing ways, according to cultural or demographic conditions, but every nation state should take ultimate responsibility in cooperation with the prompting of the leading industrial economies.

The following are some of the questions that peoples may raise in choosing to debate the problem: Should minimum age limits be set for marriage? Should compatibility tests be authorised in legalising formal unions? Should occupational divisions be made between the sexes where this is possible? Should taxation be levied on all children following the first? Should contraceptive devices be supplied free of charge by the state? Should financial inducements be made to those offering themselves for sterilisation? Should religious and secular celibate associations be established? Should erotic images or literature of any kind be suppressed (as currently in a number of Islamic states)? Should religious and other propaganda be widely circulated in emphasising the evils of materialism in contrast to spiritual values?

None of the above debatable proposals would be suitable in any ideal state, and hence should only be suggested as temporary or emergency measures in confronting the destructive threats to the planet, as well as to humankind. It is also probable that none of the tentative proposals above may be voluntarily adopted by any nation state. As so often happens in history when unpleasant choices are called for, unanticipated and unintended or accidental events may enforce a resolution to the question that is far more horrific, and welcomed by none.

The outbreak of a plague pandemic, far more fatal and contagious than Covid-19, may be cited as such an example, comparable to the Black Death in the 14th century, that may have destroyed a third or half the European population; or comparable to the Great Plague in England in 1665, being the last major out-break of the Bubonic plague, or the worldwide so-called Spanish flu epidemic of 1918-20, that killed 50,000,000, i.e., more than those slaughtered in the conflict of the First World War.

The difficulty or delay in developing vaccines is becoming ever-harder with the increasing complexity of new diseases and their mutation. Such an epidemic with the skilled population loss would lead to the breakdown of all effective communication channels and long-lasting anarchic conflict.

It may be noted that throughout the animal kingdom, population pressures in the past have often led to sudden epidemics destroying a high proportion of their species. Moreover, it has been predicted by scientists that the increasingly close connection between wild animals in captivity in the food and medical industries in the Far East, is likely sometime in the near future to trigger a major pandemic amongst humankind – as has already occurred in the past.

In regard to the self-destruction of peoples, perhaps the greatest environmental disaster of all in recent times, arising from the abuse of natural resources, is the story of the Polynesian culture of Easter island. In this instance, the story culminated in the annihilation of the greater part of the population through famine and disease. Whilst Easter island was a small universe that exhausted its resources, our planet today is relatively no less finite in the use or abuse of the environment and the consequences to follow.

CHAPTER 2
The Consequences of Over-Population

"The ultimate intelligence of our species will be determined by whether we face our population issue and get it under control, or continue to sweep it under the rug because it's an uncomfortable conversation. The future of life on Earth depends on us doing the former."

Leidani Münter, *Population Matters* website

A glance at the current population situation is necessary before any further comment or attempt to address the problem. Across the entire northern hemisphere, from Vladivostok to Reykjavik and from Hammerfest to Malta, the birth rate is collapsing amongst the ethnic peoples of the countries involved. Clearly, there is no population problem here!

On the contrary, there is the need for population increase. This is because the best educated and most socially aware peoples of the world are voluntarily eliminating themselves from the planet in their horror at what lies ahead. And this is irrespective of religion or race, for Catholics are declining no less than Protestants. The collapse of the Japanese birth rate, for example, has fallen more than in any other notable country, and yet they are amongst the best educated, and if crime statistics are taken as a guide, amongst the most law-abiding of peoples. Even in China the birth rate is declining and needs to be increased.

In the southern hemisphere, on the other hand, the increasing birth rate is out of control, as it leaps ahead, irrespective of the resources to feed an ever-poorer population. It was once argued that as soon as a population reached a sufficiently appropriate living standard, then social awareness steps in in restraining further growth. But in turning to the prosperous Arabs of the Gulf states, facts have disproved this tendency where the population is increasing on a geometrical scale in answer to the religious call of, "give birth and multiply." Even if the theory of a declining birth rate in response to increasing prosperity was true, to await such prosperity in the face of rising poverty is both a contradiction and an absurd hope.

Whilst the peoples of the northern hemisphere have a social awareness that alerts them to the need to restrict the global population; those of the south have little awareness of their long-term circumstances and are led by ancient customs and religious beliefs that exacerbate rather than resolve contemporary problems. In India and other territories, the older population is intent on ensuring as many offspring as possible, not only to offset those dying in childhood (which is rarer nowadays thanks to Western medicine) but to attend them in old age in lieu of non-existent pensions or state support.

A fatalistic attitude to every aspect of life is universal throughout Asia, and this hardens the passive acceptance of every form of suffering . The Westerner in Asia soon learns that his natural complaining instinct gets nowhere in the East, and so he quickly adopts a silent response to every irritant. The democratic traditions of the north teach the Westerner to look after his best individual interests, whilst in the south, the group looks to its narrower specific interests, whilst tending to ignore the concerns of outsiders.

In turning to the peoples of South America, it may be noted that they accept their religion in a more traditional and literal sense than their co-religionists in Europe with their more sceptical or deistic approach to church authority. Consequently, due to a combination of what can be described as nothing less

ADVANCING TECHNOLOGICAL CIVILISATION 31

than poverty and ignorance, harsh as these terms appear, birth rates race ahead, and even governments are unconcerned by climate change or threats to the environment – even going so far as to deny that such evils exist.

The first indication of these population pressures received by the peoples of the northern hemisphere, is usually via attempts of immigrants to break through national barriers in reaching prosperous territories. The total number who have so far penetrated into the north is difficult to calculate, but if border crossings from Mexico into America, or from Turkey into Greece, or from North Africa into Italy, Spain or France, or those from half way across the world to the long coast line of Australia, are taken into consideration, it amounts to tens of thousands annually.

Many claim falsely to be political refugees when in fact they are economic, and many more arrive without documentation or passports they have destroyed *en route*; and some arrive with the claim to join relatives. All apart from a tiny minority with high medical or other valued qualifications, are a financial burden on the nation states in which they arrive or eventually settle, and all contribute to unemployment figures. None have a legal right to land or settle in the northern hemisphere, or Australia or New Zealand, and their presence is only tolerated through the kindness and generosity of the peoples of the advanced Technological Civilisation. More significant, however, is the fact that those who have already penetrated, or are in the process of doing so, are a drop in the ocean by comparison with the numbers that would arrive if they pushed their determination sufficiently to do so.

The arrival of 10,000 per year may seem a modest number, but what if half a million were to arrive within a 5-year period, and that is a possibility, bearing in mind the rapidly changing demographics of the world situation? This reason, based on fairness to the peoples of both north and south in anticipating existing intentions, is a sufficient argument for barring any further attempts at immigration except in extraordinary circumstances.

In Brazil we witness the destruction of the world's largest rainforest – the lung of the world – and the situation has been worsened at the behest of recently elected governments to hasten the process of burning and clearing the rainforest in preparation for farmland and the breeding of cattle. The short-termism of the policy is emphasised by the fact that after several years the poor soil will be so denuded as to be useless for agriculture. In Indonesia and elsewhere, similar policies are pursued in destroying the natural environment and the extermination of many species, as huge mining projects or palm oil or soya plantations replace the ancient and globally beneficial woodland for a healthy planet.

In view of these damaging policies, undertaken in response to uncontrollable population increases – although the latter is rarely referred to directly – it is difficult to find an answer as to how such a doom-laden fate may be avoided. The problem is international or global as a possibly permanent or irreversible threat to all life on the planet, but needs to be addressed separately by each offending nation state according to its specific situation. It is not simply a question of halting population growth, but of population *reduction*. To address the question of population reduction is already a provocative proposition, but to carry it out in action is far more so. The reiteration of the spoken word, or warnings, or vague threats, from whomsoever or whatever representative group, is not sufficient.

The problem calls for a powerfully organised body carrying the moral authority of those with a different mindset, and a different way of living, and this can only be realised

ADVANCING TECHNOLOGICAL CIVILISATION

through a federation of states as described in the previous chapter. It is not suggested that such a body should necessarily employ force in achieving its objectives, but it is necessary that it should possess the potential to exert such force. And that is the reason why the strongest industrial economies should unite with the assertion of claiming a dominating role over all other territories for a world-saving purpose. Such leading advocates of our Technological Civilisation would need to concentrate on every aspect of the beneficent claim in identifying their purpose, from every ethical and practical angle.

Such practical steps would undoubtedly provoke resistance from varying directions on the grounds of "legality." What right would such a suddenly emerging body have to exist in the first place? What right would any association have to assert its dominion as a rightfully advanced organisation, howsoever justified over others? To what extent would such a body trespass or trample on the business of other long-established associations, such as the United Nations or any of its subsidiary departments? Such justification would only be found in two arguments: firstly, that no existing organisation is sufficiently competent to halt permanent and life-threatening dangers to the planet; and secondly, in asserting the moral right of might as the only remaining practical course in the face of such a crisis. Hence, if there is a clash between the international legislation of such a newly proposed organisation with those already in existence, then the former should be made to prevail.

The first step of the proposed Tripartite Alliance should be the declaration that each nation state is ultimately responsible for its own welfare and best interests, and this should entail population control, and when necessary, population reduction. In those countries where the population increase is clearly out of control, or where it is already far in excess of desirable resources to maintain such a population, then the second step is that international legislation should be passed in forbidding the emigration of nationals from such territories. If such offending nation states contravene the above or other regulations, then the third step would entail international legislation restricting trade.

Although armed force, or the threat of such, should not be used against territories solely on the grounds of excess populations, or those who fail for any reason to fulfil other regulations imposed; in the event of positive action in harming the environment, e.g., destroying the rainforest or establishing palm oil or soya plantations or other agricultural projects on land previously part of the rainforest, then a stronger response should be called for. In other words, a distinction should be made between ills that arise through a negative or positive situation. In the latter, as such evils are intentionally created that may destroy animal life on the planet, the threat or actuality of armed force should in extreme cases be held in reserve.

In every nation state, it should be acknowledged, there would be some who were sufficiently socially aware, or informed, or educated, to be in *active* sympathy with the purposes of advanced Technological Civilisation, and such individuals or groups should be granted full membership of the Tripartite Alliance, and act as appointed agents for their respective countries. In that role, the aims of the association should then be achieved through friendly cooperation without undue external pressure. The eventual aim would be to include ever-more nation states into the Tripartite Alliance so that eventually all the world would be included in contributing to the leading purposes of Technological Civilisation.

CHAPTER 3
The Road to Progress

"I've seen melting ice caps with my own eyes and got wet in the process. But, as a passionate promoter of economic, social and environmental sustainability, it is pointless campaigning against climate change or to 'Save the Arctic' without addressing the root cause behind it and virtually every other environmental or indeed social issue we face: our unsustainability numbers on this planet. That is the real inconvenient truth."

Adrian Hayes, on video & *Population Matters* website

If the above summarises the external threats to Technological Civilisation, and how they may be countered through appropriate planning, we must now turn to the more immediate and greater internal threats. These are primarily from the loss of belief in Technological Civilisation, not so much due to mistrust of material progress as through half-hidden suggestions of guilt as participants of an all-powerful civilisation that may or seemingly somehow threaten those from less fortunate cultures.

These feelings are manifested or directed in a variety of ways: e.g., in questioning that a degree of value may be measured between peoples, nations, cultures, or civilisations; repudiating the historical significance of the past; disdaining all aspects of colonialism; undermining an objective view of our place in the universe; mistrust of competition; the dislike of achievement by those regarded as privileged; resentment of leadership howsoever expressed; or reluctance to recognise the underlying motivations of social prosperity, etc. Such loss of self-assurance within the social environment of one's birth leads inevitably to differing modes of thought with consequences destructive to society.

This brings into prominence the need to describe how civilisations emerge and flourish for the longer term. Pre-civilisational societies comprise a mix of innumerable tribes that exists in a state of almost constant war. Historically, this may be found in every part of the globe as an intrinsic part of human nature at a certain stage of evolutionary development. Just as characteristics of behaviour are similar everywhere, so likewise are thought processes and the pattern of myths, stories, and dreams, which are repeated globally from the primitive tribes of the Pacific or those of Asia, Europe, or any part of America. Sir James Frazer has studied these repetitive patterns in depth in a number of voluminous works.

With the development of humankind from hunter-gatherers to the more settled existence of agricultural communities, and later, into city complexes, social conflict is greatly diminished through the fore-thought and longer time-span entailed in farming, and the division of labour involved in the manufacture of tangibles. Nonetheless, all change, howsoever beneficent from an objective standpoint, is in some degree painful to significant population sectors, and consequently is resisted in giving rise to conflict.

Whilst in primitive societies, conflict may be greater between rather than within communities, in more advanced or sophisticated cultures, the opposite may prevail. This is not to suggest that underlying or open conflict is not frequent between all contiguous civilisations and cultures as a natural and inescapable human tendency. Difference in itself, in its changing degrees, gives ground for conflict. Most conflict between peoples arise from economic causes, through population pressures, or changes in the availability of water resources, or the depletion of good agricultural land, or competition for markets, etc., but such causes are often disguised, or even hidden entirely from those involved at the time, by cultural factors as religion, language, nationality or race.

The most frequent cause of civilisational conflict arises from the inequality of peoples. That is, more materially advanced civilisations, which almost invariably are also the most culturally developed, have a tendency (even if unintended) to extend their boundaries. Such extension may initially be welcomed by less enlightened peoples, until they are suddenly awoken to the awareness of injustice or oppression. The contiguity between higher civilisations, on the other hand, usually leads to a spirit of tolerance and compromise on both sides, whilst each safeguards its integrity through wariness and distance.

A close study of history over the past 5,000 years clearly demonstrates the material and cultural development of humankind, although even leading civilisations may be struck down by decline and decadence. It is then that progress may be stopped in its tracks – sometimes for centuries, until recovery through the inspiration of an ancient past allows humankind to once again take up the baton for advancement. Hence progress for most of history has been a process of stops and starts, and it is only during the past 500 years that civilisation has shot ahead with a speed and velocity unknown before. This has been achieved through the rise and success of Western Civilisation, which should now more appropriately be referred to as Technological Civilisation in deference to the Confucian cultures of the Far East.

To raise the question as to whether civilisations have the right to expansion is an absurdity in view of the fact that their influence is an inevitable process of human development. The greatest reality of civilisations, or cultures, or animal life in its entirety, is in its inequality. Every species has its pecking order, expressed in a variety of ways. The concept of *difference* is sometimes used in place of *equality* as a gentler mode of expression, but the two are not the same in any proper sense. The material status of a civilisation is usually but not invariably linked to a similar level of its cultural development, and for this reason has less motivation to question its rightful place or superiority amongst surrounding cultures or peoples.

The trading and other relationships between civilisations and cultures in a colonial or imperial environment, will inescapably arouse some misunderstanding and tensions during the earlier years, decades, or even centuries of contact, since none can guess the mindset or behaviour of the other, or have the ability to interpret such. Such mutual ignorance often breaks into open conflict, and occasionally, even into criminal outrages from either side which only time can heal. The expansion of a dominating civilisation, however mild or tactful its intentions, is bound at some point to arouse resentment, even if the latter is hidden behind a mask of civility.

On balance, it should be recognised that the domination of leading civilisations throughout every era of history has usually resulted in a benign outcome for all those involved. This is because higher levels of material and intellectual standards are everywhere valued, and after a period of doubt or resistance, are eventually accepted in their entirety by subordinated peoples in contributing to their greater improvement and happiness. How else could progress have been achieved? Despite the heavy loss of life and suffering that peoples in central Europe may have endured during the pre-Empire (status) Roman period, the former were eventually to inherit and create the greatest civilisation the world has known. And this would not have been possible without the traditions of administration, law, philosophy, and culture that was transmitted by Romano-Hellenic civilisation to those they subordinated. The same comparisons may be said of modern history, although we shall have more to say on this in a later chapter.

Every civilisation and culture flourishes within its own sphere in defining and limiting its existence. If these limits are undermined or compromised, the culture may be harmed or destroyed. The higher the culture, the more resistant it naturally is to the possibility of such threats. And this is the reason why so many primitive cultures – and in great part their peoples – have been quickly destroyed through contact with more technically powerful forces. The original ethnic populations of North America, Australia, and other Pacific regions come immediately to mind. Such destruction has not occurred through intentional measures, but rather due to the side-lining of such peoples, in the ordinary course of developing agriculture or urban areas. The actual destruction of such peoples has usually arisen through alcoholism or drug addiction, and the breakdown of traditional values in the failed attempt to integrate with modern ways of living.

In regard to contact between powerful forces and cultures occupying an intermediate level of civilisation, such as India and other territories in the East, other problems will occur. In developing trading relationships with India, Britain (or the East India Company) has never seriously attempted to impose her own values on an already established civilisation, although in the 1830s, a national newspaper, administration, and educational system along Western lines, were introduced in more closely unifying the country with the imperial power. Such measures were hardly resisted, and alongside the technological development of railways, etc., were eventually adopted as intrinsic to the Indian way of life. In travelling to the East, I have always found Indians to be proud of their

British connection, and happy to promote the interests of British trade.

France and the Netherlands adopted similar policies in their respective territories, and whilst France emphasised the importance of her culture as an essential aspect of civilisation; the Netherlands may have imposed too strong a form of bureaucracy that aroused resentment. All such imperial or colonial measures, irrespective of their long-term beneficence, were destined to last for a limited period until such countries were sufficiently prepared for independence. Again, this is a subject to which we shall return in a later chapter.

The sphere in which any culture, or nation state exists, needs to be respected, and this has been followed by the European powers in regard to cultures on an intermediate level. The same can hardly be said in regard to Europe's relationship with less developed peoples. Here, the situation has been difficult due to the lack of understanding, and the huge change required in developing a fair system of trade and modern infrastructures to accommodate the same. In Africa, especially, major difficulties and even atrocities have followed in the wake of European contact – not necessarily through the responsibility of nation states, but through the initiative of powerful individuals working on their own behalf.

Consequently, the independent emergence of nation states that have more recently arisen in Africa often remain in a state of internal conflict. This has been partly due to frontiers crossing through tribal areas, giving rise to language and cultural differences as a cause for bloody conflict; and partly through the lack of educational development enabling popular or democratic government. The unnatural national frontiers arose through the arbitrary division of territory by the imperial powers; whilst poor material development was due to the reluctance of Europeans in sufficient numbers to settle in an often unpleasant climate.

A glance at recoded history clearly demonstrates the technological and intellectual advance of humankind on a global scale, but during that intervening period, it also demonstrates the inequality of peoples, as otherwise such progress would not and could not have been achieved. Resistance by the subordinated has proven that progress is a painful process, but once achieved it is not only accepted as a benefit, but also in the equalising of peoples towards a common level of opportunity and justice.

The above clearly shows that the role of the European powers in disseminating civilisation throughout the world, is one for pride and celebration, rather than regret. The closing decades of imperialism were troubled years of confusion and mis-judged decision-making, for which the littoral European powers were not entirely to blame. There always had been episodes of conflict, and occasionally outrages, both of which were often unintended or accidental, but nonetheless, progress continued to be carried forward to the benefit of colonial peoples. The factor that cast a dark shadow over the final years of imperialism was the indecent haste to shed responsibility.

There were two causes for this: firstly, the weakened economic situation of Europe at the close of World War II, and the costs of maintaining advisory and administrative civil servants abroad; and secondly, the political pressure of America in opposing the idea of European imperialism under any circumstances. During the Second World War in America, there were leading statesmen and leading military personnel who secretly held the opinion that the War was not merely against the Fascist axis powers, but more broadly against the general tendency of what they regarded as European expansionism.

This was the second time during the 20th century when the isolationist peace-loving American people had been reluctantly dragged into a worldwide conflict, and they resented that part of the world they felt was ultimately responsible. Their resentment may have been surprising in view of their own imperial venture in 1998 with its profitable outcome, but that episode had been quickly forgotten. Most shocking at the time was when Churchill's "best friend," Franklin D. Roosevelt, had his *tête-à-tête* with Stalin on how best to approach European imperialism at the end of the War.

The consequence was that the independence of almost all colonies was granted prematurely, leading to botched solutions, and sometimes to bloodshed on a massive scale, as in India. Had another decade been allowed to lapse, a much happier outcome might have resulted, leaving better memories for both the European powers and their former territories.

CHAPTER 4
The Vulnerability of Civilisations

"There is nothing so fragile as civilisation, and no civilisation has long withstood the manifold risks it is exposed to."

Havelock Ellis, *Impressions and Comments*, Ser. I, p. 105.

It is now necessary to consider the vulnerability of all leading civilisations during the period of their predominance, and their liability to decline and fall. As we have explained above, every civilisation exists within its own cultural sphere that acts as a unique creative and unifying force, or life-blood, in assuring its healthy progress in warding off symptoms of social disease or degeneration.

The life force of any civilisation or culture is difficult to define with precision, but many cultures have cherished a clear image of those virtues contributing to their rise and maintaining their stability. It is easier, however, to identify those characteristics contributing to the decline of civilisations.

Most common is the immigration of great numbers of those from a foreign clime, followed by their high birth rates and failure to integrate with the ethnic population. This certainly was a major contributing factor to the decline and fall of Rome, due to the huge immigration of peoples from the East and North who eventually found themselves in leading administrative, military, and government positions, as the birth rate of the original population collapsed. The latter problem was addressed by its first Emperor, Augustus, who strove to encourage marriage on a more widespread scale, but sadly, his efforts were unheeded. Meanwhile, Roman citizenship was granted to an ever-widening circle of the population with little regard to cultural factors.

Rapid changes to the structure and character of society were bound to exert a conflict of values leading to the breakdown of creative motivations upholding the culture. The Romans of the later Republican and Imperial periods had a clear vision of the qualities that upheld their civilisation. They looked back to the virtues of a simpler and harder life, committed to the ideal of service, and free from the corrupting influence of peoples to the East. The voice of the unrelenting Cato the Elder, was repeated throughout the centuries, with his warning against the dangers of "foreign ways."

Of equal, if not greater harm in undermining Roman civilisation was the accelerating polarisation of wealth and land ownership, leading to the decline of agriculture and increasing dependence on imported grain from Egypt and other parts of North Africa. This was accompanied by unemployment on a massive scale, and dependence on the dole, or what became the creation of a "welfare state." The manumission of slaves only added to the problem, for whilst they had work and often enjoyed greater prosperity than "free men," their manumission cast them adrift from the security of a guaranteed livelihood.

The polarisation of wealth into the hands of an exclusive super-rich, often with few responsibilities to society, eventually led to the contraction of the army, and the ruin of productive business due to taxation rates that became intolerable. At that stage, the Empire was an invitation to the barbarian hordes to invade. If the above is a reminder of contemporary conditions nearer home, then it stands as a warning for our own future. There are occasions when history is repeated as a moral lesson or benefit for peoples of the centuries or even millennia ahead.

At this stage, it would be useful to look a little more closely at how the word "Civilisation" is used at the present time. The most comprehensive or practical interpretation of civilisation was probably given by Arnold Toynbee in his 12-

volume work, *A Study of History*. He identified 25 civilisations that have existed in the world from the earliest recorded times until the present (i.e. 1954), and he analysed their rise through a process of challenge and response, and their disintegration through Schism in the Body Social and Schism in the Soul. In addition, he studied arrested civilisations, and the nature of contact between civilisations in space and time.

When the word civilisation is used in the singular, it usually refers to our Western Civilisation as traceable to the Greeks, and further back, and to the monotheistic influences of the Near East through the growth of Christianity. It may be noted, however, that Kenneth Clark, author of the renowned TV series, *A History of Civilisation*, has been misjudged on two quite separate counts: firstly, in that his approach avoided sufficient breadth in covering the topic; and secondly, that he embarked on a singular rather than a plural title and approach. In a further gesture of malice, critics (with a questionable agenda of their own) have remarked that he was "old-fashioned" and "conventional," although in the view of Huw Wheldon "it was a truly great series, a major work ... the first magnum opus attempted and realised in terms of TV," whilst John Betjeman described Clark as, "the man who made the best telly you've ever seen."

We see here, a contrast between those with the secret intention of undermining the status of Western Civilisation as being "one amongst equals," and those who truly comprehend its unique significance as a giant step towards the progress of humankind. The epithets, "old-fashioned" or "conventional" as critical terms, are anyway meaningless, since they have no factual reference to a measurement of value. One could just as well argue that Plato, Shakespeare, or Mozart, were "old-fashioned" and attempt to call that criticism.

The real issue that a widening circle of contemporary critics have with Kenneth Clark, and others, therefore, is that the study of civilisation should only be made in the plural in indicating that no civilisation should rightfully be portrayed as being "better" than another. And the reasoning for this is that reference to or emphasis on the existence of Western (or Technological) Civilisation, might give offence to a person of colour from sub-Saharan Africa, or New Guinea, or Bangladesh, or elsewhere through inferring that their civilisations might somehow be "inferior." Such patronising nonsense, of course, is insulting to Africans or the peoples of New Guinea or Bangladesh. These peoples may and should be loyal to and love their own cultures whilst also freely acknowledging the higher status of another.

There is no conflict of interest here, but merely the common sense realisation that differing levels of values are a reality of existence. It would be unrealistic of Africans and others to deny the material benefits of medicine, electricity, transport, and better housing, etc., as not being indebted to a superior or more distant civilisation. And such benefits need not be in a one-way direction. In exchange, the peoples of the advanced Technological Civilisation may equally welcome the arts, music, and other products of developing peoples - as they already do. All exchange enhances mutual understanding.

Those who believe, or at least, declare that all things are of equal value or deserving of equal attention within and beyond our Technological Civilisation, are stupefied by the overwhelming significance of the latter to such a degree they cannot cope with the apparent responsibility it seems to suggest. They are overcome with a mixture of guilt and humility, and desire to reduce themselves to a lower or more equal level to those they would embrace as brothers and sisters. Laudable as such feelings may appear, they present a distorted perspective of the wider world, and such people would better project themselves as teachers or purveyors of knowledge from their own culture, than in the useless role of diminished equals.

A more dangerous attitude of such a mindset by those attempting to adjust their relationship with those from less privileged cultures, is the open encouragement of the latter, for it diverts attention away from the more immediate priority of integration into the new society. Such an attitude is not in the best interests of people of colour, as they are driven back to their origins instead of forward to the hope of a better future. In other words, through the purpose of what is now described as *diversity*, a further divide is driven between alternative ways of living, or how the latter is appreciated. Such distance increases rather than decreases cultural misunderstanding. Such encouragement of *diversity* may have a generous intention but it is not understood or appreciated by those nearby and further afield who, in a busy world, are only concerned with their ordinary lives and accepted standards.

If an African, or for that matter, anyone from a far flung region, is culturally fully integrated into a European environment, in terms of speech, thought or behaviour, his colour will be of no significance beyond the incidental, for he will be fully accepted as having *no differences* as an equal. This is currently the situation in both Britain and America, and most places throughout the world. If there is still divisiveness, and there is, this is the fault of contemporary forms of ghettoization, and the retention of foreign ways, either intentionally or unconsciously imposed. Racial mixing, either biologically or socially, eliminates racial consciousness in contributing to a friendlier and more stable society, and so inter-marriage between ethnic populations and immigrants, when the opportunity arises, should be encouraged in helping to culturally integrate the latter.

48   ADVANCING TECHNOLOGICAL CIVILISATION

Those who allegedly befriend immigrant populations by pushing them back into their less enlightened cultures, therefore harm their future prospects rather than promote them. Their falsely generated guilt at what they feel is their privileged position, not only drives them towards all manner of *diversity* polices, but to disdain their own kind along whom they were nurtured. These are the same people who rail against those whom they pejoratively describe as "White, middle class, and middle-aged," as if those were characteristics to be disdained.

But their success in tarnishing the reputation of so large a proportion of the British ethnic population has been widespread, and even caught the attention of the media for even wider circulation. The victims of this senseless and unjust abuse are unable to respond, for they cannot issue a denial any more than a person of African descent may deny he is black. Why, then, has the abuse occurred in the first place? It is merely an expression of resentment against those imagined to be privileged and also as those alleged to discriminate, on occasion, against the immigrant community.

What is the true reality in most accurately describing those amongst our population who are, "White, middle class and middle-aged"? They in fact comprise the best educated, most qualified, experienced, and due to their years, most sagacious sector of the population. Those who thoughtlessly propagate such slander do not deserve to claim the citizenship or nationality of the country that has sustained them. The slogan is a subtle and cleverly concealed attack on everything that represents the British character and psyche. Of most significance is the fact that that those who blacken the reputation of others in this way, are not only hypocrites but guilty of a type of racism as bad as any other.

If advanced Technological Civilisation, through the Tripartite Alliance is to assume a dominating position in the world, it can only justify such a role if internally its mode of government and social purpose is justice as fairness in promoting both majority interests and those of minorities.

At the present time, there are several factors limiting such a possibility, and these must be addressed. There are, of course, questions in regard to China's treatment of certain minorities, but in the West, there are two far greater problems: firstly, the degeneration and impending collapse of democracy as we know it in its present form; and secondly, a financial-industrial system that is polarising wealth and undermining the interests of the emerging middle majority. As it is the last factor that is threatening democracy as we know it, we must now turn to considering the financial situation as a preliminary step.

CHAPTER 5
The Fatal Flaw of the Financial System

"As the soaring demand for food, water and energy is exacerbated by climate change, it is no longer legitimate to leave policies for lowering birth rates off the policy agenda."

Sara Parkin, OBE, *Population Matters* website

The myopia of Western peoples – or at least, those of America and Britain – to the self-destructiveness of the financial-industrial system is hardly to be credited. But cultures are often unaware of obvious threats lying at their feet. This is because what is taken for granted as part of the natural environment is rarely questioned – or even noticed.

One of the great ironies of our time is the economic blame that America casts on China for its own miserable economic record, and this is because America's degeneration is entirely self-inflicted. There was a 30-year period following the establishment of Communism in China, when she had little or no interest in trading with the West.

It was America that wanted to trade with the great power in the Far East and open up her market. Shortly before becoming President in 1969, Richard Nixon had written in the *Foreign Affairs* journal that, "There is no place on this small planet for a billion of its potentially most able people to live in angry isolation," and in 1972, he made his famous visit to Chairman Mao Zedong and Premier Zhou Enlai. This was the start of approaches to develop trade, which was not seriously embarked upon until after 1978 with the accession to power of Deng Ziaoping, and his extensive economic reforms.

The response of the financial-industrial establishment in America was to fully exploit this situation to their own financial benefit. As the priority of American business had increasingly been interpreted as the maximising of investors' profits, this entailed seeking lower-cost markets in which to manufacture their own products. There was therefore no hesitation amongst leading industrialists, i.e., the actual owners of corporate stock market led business (as opposed to those manufacturing at plant level) to seize the opportunities that China offered.

Over a period of time, as investors increased their profits through overseas operations whilst home-based industry declined year by year, millions of Americans were either unemployed or pushed into lower paid occupations. The dire economic situation was, of course, compounded by the fact of the re-importation of American owned but Chinese manufactured products, for all imports entail a cost, and in excess, they contribute to the overall imbalance of trade.

Hence, in glancing at the overall situation, there is clearly a conflict of interest between investors (or owners) and those at plant level who actually contribute their technical, inventive, and other skills in the practical business of manufacturing, marketing and selling. This is a social and economic divide that is hardly if ever mentioned either within or outside business circles.

It is never discussed within business circles for the obvious reason that the Chief Executive Officers at plant level – irrespective of the grand titles they may use, as Chairman, Managing Director, etc., - are dependent on accountancy factors beyond their control. Moreover, they are usually frightened men (and far less usually women), who are disciplined employees, and may be immediately removed from their relatively well-paid positions for noises indicating the existence of an unpleasant or embarrassing situation.

Everyone employed in business is aware that it must exist *as it is* and not as it *should be*, for there is no activity where money-power exerts a greater pressure on the lone individual. This aspect of money-power is not discussed outside business circles for the obvious reason that nobody is interested in something that is not directly their concern, although clearly within the remit of others.

From the above, it may be seen that America's resentful blame of China for her wretched economic situation is not only misplaced but ridiculous. The blame lies on the shoulders of American financiers, alongside the cooperation of their corporations, in bringing ruin to the nation state. There is, therefore, a conflict of interest between international and national interests, and this has been made possible over so long a period because the financial-industrial institutions are not accountable to democratic control or correction.

The cry of Margaret Thatcher, Ronald Reagan, and others, supported by a powerful economic lobby, most notably by the monetarists, Milton Friedman and Alan Walters, that business should remain separate from government, was always a malign conviction. This is not only because business, in the guise of high finance, may often evade taxation through hiding in offshore locations, and engaging in other skulduggery, but for the reason as cited above in exploiting the divide between investors and home-based productivity.

There is, of course, a better alternative long proven in serving national interests defined in terms of greater benefit to the majority. And that is the social democratic model, as demonstrated by the north western European Continental countries and the Far East Tigers in the decades following the Second World War. This, Productive mode of capitalism, not only vastly out-competed the Rentier capitalist economies of Britain and America in capturing overseas markets, but also in everywhere ensuring a more equal distribution of wealth throughout society.

It is no wonder that Rentier capitalism, based on the narrow rationale of maximising investors' profits, is ultimately self-destructive since its purpose ignores the first priority of business which surely should be in best serving consumers' interests through maximising commercially viable productivity. The making of money out of money leads to usury, or the loss of proper connection between investment and productivity. These are better understood through explaining the differing modes of investment between Rentier and Productive capitalism.

The Rentier mode is dependent on large-scale corporative or stock exchange investment, often involving conglomerates owning and controlling a huge portfolio of enterprises of every conceivable kind. Under this system, investors are brought together not to promote specific businesses in which they have a particular interest, but any business that seems to offer a better or quicker return. Under such a system, investing activity changes frequently between one company and another, so that few businesses can rely on the loyalty of their backers for any length of time. This naturally contributes to the feeling of uncertainty or insecurity within enterprises which in turn leads to reluctance to innovate or expand.

Worse still, under such a system where the investor is King, business may be divided into category types where some bring quicker or higher returns than others according to the technological complexity or necessary costs of the company. It is no surprise, therefore, that manufacturing is generally the most discriminated against, as the demand for innovation and growth in keeping apace with the latest developments of the competition, frighten those investors away who are intent on a quicker profit. As manufacturing is the most important sector of business, as it is the most technologically advanced in maintaining the standards of any civilisation, it clearly fails to fit in comfortably with the Rentier economies of Britain and America. And the record of recent history has amply proven this.

If we turn to the Productive mode of capitalism, we uncover a very different situation. The typical mode of funding business is through the existence of Industrial investment credit banks, with a sound knowledge of the technical and marketing potential of specific enterprises, and so embracing the ability to lend long term at low interest rates. Via this system, Bank Directors are often appointed to the board of companies where they perform the equivalent function of Financial directors as found within the Rentier management system. But whilst Financial Directors within the Rentier company are guided towards utilising internal resources, i.e., the repair of existing machinery, with an eye on cutting out seemingly unnecessary costs; the Bank Director facilitates unlimited (but controlled) lending in enabling modernisation and expansion.

It is true that under this system, the company is placed in the pocket of the bank, but on the other hand, it is allowed to maximise its service to the consumer and meet international competition from any quarter. Under Productive capitalism, independent or family-sized business is more commonly retained, and all business is more secure in relation to its future since it is not exposed to the casino-environment of a usurious financial system. Stock exchange activity naturally operates alongside and in cooperation with industrial investment credit banks (which are non-existent in the Rentier economy), but such stock exchanges have a very different culture from those of Wall Street or London.

This is not to criticise the stock exchange activity of the latter in any absolute sense, since they developed with the primary purpose of promoting international or colonial trade, and the high risks of foreign ventures – especially those traceable to earlier centuries – justified high interest rates to cover such eventualities. The British stock exchange, for example, played a negligible role in the early development of industry which was financed by private capital or by the hundreds of provincial banks that once existed until the close of the 19th century.

It should be understood that Rentier and Productive capitalism developed in differing circumstances in different eras. British capitalism is traceable to the sack of the monasteries in the 1530s, and the trading environment that grew from this through the rising middle classes under the patronage of Henry VIII in strengthening his own power in balance against the older nobility. The founding of various trading companies and the growth of shipping for trade, and the intensification of competition for markets leading eventually to piracy (to which the state attempted to turn a blind eye), led to unprecedented personal wealth, which in combination with inventiveness in a free society, triggered the industrial revolution in the 18th century.

Britain's domination in all sectors of manufacturing by the middle of the 19th century posed a problem that could not be easily overcome by the rest of Europe. Personal financial wealth was insufficient to develop large scale industry on two counts: firstly, in that it was far less widespread than in Britain; and secondly, because the complexity of technology had by that time developed to a prohibitive cost for individual investment, business was obliged to turn to the state for assistance. The response was a new economic philosophy that conflicted with *laissez-faire*.

This was a question of the national protectionist economics of Friedrich List, versus the free market ideas of

Adam Smith – each ideally suited to the respective demands of their time. The state was called upon to initiate the founding of industrial investment credit banks; technical institutes; and protective measures against foreign competition. The repercussion of these startling and provocative strategies – condemned in Britain as contrary to "proper" business principles – was in part responsible for growing tension between Britain and Imperial Germany at the start of the 20th century.

The real economic significance between these two forms of capitalism did not become apparent until the decades following World War II. It may therefore be asked in a social democratic world that had then developed, if Productive capitalism was more socially beneficial in equally distributing the sources of wealth, then why did it not prevail over the Rentier model? There are a number of answers to this question.

Firstly, living standards everywhere shot ahead in the advanced industrial economies, irrespective of economic or manufacturing success. For example, if manufacturing accelerated at 10% per year in Continental Europe or amongst the Far East Tigers, whilst in Britain it remained at 2%, the latter was nonetheless judged a success – or at least satisfactory – due to the complacency generated by rising living standards. In other words, the latter concealed the differences between relative and total values.

Secondly, the Cold War concentrated divisions in society as not those between capitalistic systems, but rather those between *laissez-faire* capitalism and totalitarian Communism. When American commentators did on the rare occasion turn their attention to the role of Productive capitalism, which they described as the Social Democratic model, they simply dismissed it as not "proper capitalism."

ADVANCING TECHNOLOGICAL CIVILISATION 57

Thirdly, from the 1980s onwards, the American style of Rentier capitalism began to dominate throughout the Western world, as well as amongst the Far East Tigers. It was with the emergence of Thatcherism that Britain was used as a launching pad for America to penetrate the Continental countries of Europe; and it was in response to that that the eminent economist, Michel Albert, the Permanent Secretary of the Académie des Sciences Morales et Politiques, published his book, *Capitalisme contre Capitalisme*, in Paris in 1991, as a warning to the Productive economies in their social democratic societies of the dangers ahead. The terms that Albert used in differentiating between the two systems were Neo-American capitalism versus the Rhine mode of capitalism – the latter to include the Far East Tigers.

Unfortunately, the book had little influence in holding back the tidal force of American power. Whilst in Japan, the economy was reduced to the verge of ruin during the 1990s, in Europe, the Continental countries have stood their ground to a certain degree until the present time. The success of America was not merely due to its sheer might, or ideological appeal, but far more significantly to the sudden rising competitive power of China. If Western industry could not compete, then business people were persuaded to look towards new ways of generating profit. And this was obviously to transfer manufacturing to overseas locations and enjoy the profits generated by foreign workers.

Nonetheless, despite these changes, there still remains a sharp distinction between Anglo-American business and that of Continental Europe or the Far East Tigers of Japan or Korea. In Germany, France, Scandinavia, etc., there is far more protectionism or state aid for industry than in Britain or America – even when EU rules are seemingly broken. In Britain, everything is "up for sale," and what is described as promoting the principles of a "free market," is in fact accelerating economic ruin. This is not only brought about by the decline of manufacturing jobs, and the loss of skills essential for a technological civilisation, but through surrendering essential utilities to foreign ownership and the vulnerability this bring to the economy of any nation state.

The mechanisms of the Anglo-American or Rentier mode of capitalism in reality contradicts entirely its ideological principles as being democratically accountable. It is neither free nor just in impacting on the majority. This is because the usurious trap into which it has fallen polarises wealth, diminishes the range of ownership, and destroys desirable types of competition. Its freedom is only perceived through its internationalism in defying the democratic accountability of nation states, through tax evasion, skulduggery in offshore hideouts, and undermining home-based products through the waste of extravagant or unnecessary transport costs of goods that benefit traders but cannot otherwise be justified.

If American capitalism is still able to maintain its shine as an ideological attraction with the majority, this is only because it is confronted by a still greater evil, viz., socialism. Socialism has always been cursed by an anti-business ethos. Business should not only be profitable, but always seek to maximise profitability, but *only* within the social purpose of promoting productivity. It is these factors that have never been properly clarified, and to which we must now turn in considering the present crisis of democracy.

CHAPTER 6
The Threat to Western Democracy

"Population was a big issue about 30 years ago, now it's not, but suspect it will come back because it has to be discussed as one of the big environmental problems of our time, it's one animal species out of control, and the awful thing is that if we don't control it then Mother Nature will do it for us."

Sir Crispen Tickell, Director of *Policy Foresight Programme* & *Population Matters* website

Democracy in both the ancient and modern world, which has always been a delicate plant, only arises in commercially active societies that have reached a certain level of development. Today we associate free market capitalism (howsoever interpreted) with a democratic society, and find it difficult to imagine one without the other.

We contrast such a society with the totalitarianism of socialism in its extreme form, as in the Soviet east until 1989, or with military or other dictatorships based on privileged elites, as commonly found in central or south America at the present time, with their ungovernable economies or hyper-inflation. Whilst socialism appears in differing degrees from mild (at the liberal end) to extreme, its logical progression is always towards the latter.

As a form of government, it ultimately exerts a malign influence as it cannot evade its anti-business ethos, or inability to appreciate the need for the dynamism of the business instinct. Its suspicion, or misinterpretation, or mis-understanding of profit will always ensure its eventual downfall as a successful form of government. That is why in successful societies, it can only survive when balanced against the strong opposition of other parties, or the existence of a capitalist system that cannot easily be evaded as the dominating influence.

Today, in the advanced industrial economies, there is little threat from socialism, but both governmental democracy and capitalism are confronted by crises that threaten their existence. The two threats are interconnected, but in examining the problem, we must first turn to the transformation of society over the past 60 years. The structure of society has changed from a top-down pyramid of split interests between a middle and upper class with its own ideals and interests, versus a working class or proletariat which experienced oppression; to an egg-shaped structure standing on its thicker end, with a new middle majority.

The new middle majority has emerged through the growth of egalitarianism, in conjunction with the development of a more complex technological civilisation calling for far greater brainpower than hitherto. Hence, there has been an upward movement of the working class, and a downward movement of those from the upper levels.

The cultural consequences of this have been considerable. Whilst the middle classes have lost (or are fast losing) their sense of pride and exclusivity – and even their sense of class; the old working class having risen in status and material achievement, have lost the resentment that once divided society. A society that once admitted only 2% of the population to a university education, now admits little short of 50%. Meanwhile, many middle layers of management have disappeared, and a far closer knowledge base brings those at the apex and base of skills into a closer relationship.

There is no room here for claims to privilege based on meritocracy, except for those risking ridicule or contempt.

ADVANCING TECHNOLOGICAL CIVILISATION

Whilst the super-rich may represent 2 ½% of the population, and a mixture of unfortunates for a variety of reasons from every sector of the community represent 7 ½%, the bulk of the population form an increasingly homogeneous majority. This is not to suggest that the middle majority comprise an absolute equality, for the latter is both indefinable and impossible, but it does indicate a political and social equality in terms of fairness and justice.

Equality is indefinable within a free society due to the variety of ways in which an individual may use his financial resources. Whilst those of middling income may spend their resources in such a way as to convey considerable luxury or wealth; there are also those amongst the super-rich who are so miserly they convey an impression of living in penury. The condition of a free society is that any individual may choose to live in any way he chooses, and this acts as a cover in diminishing the appearance of any remaining evidence of inequality.

The political system based on the mechanism of the left/right divide, in advancing democracy and pushing progress forward, has not kept apace with the reality of events. It has remained trapped ideologically in a time-warp of the past. Hence, the left/right struggle has become meaningless in interpreting the world as we know it today, and so the socially aware, or those of good nature, are disgusted by appeals that are not merely made to their baser instincts but to a fraudulent presentation of actuality. Why should we loathe those who were once superior, but with whom we are now equal; or despise those who were once inferior, but may now be better than ourselves? Disgust with politicians, and even more with the deceitful ideologies they seek to impose, has led to the crash of all established party political memberships, and to voting figures also, throughout the advanced industrial economies.

This is not to suggest that politicians are so purblind as not to recognise the changing situation of society, but as party members, bound by obedience to their leadership, they cannot escape the defining parameters of the cause. Their response to this differs according to circumstance. Many declare their repudiation, or temporary suspension of belief in ideology in opting for a pragmatic approach which may compound their difficulties. This is because pragmatism takes every issue in isolation as a thing in itself, unconnected with any general principle, and hence puts a greater distance between the politician and the electorate.

The pragmatic policy may be any idea plucked out of the sky, and such ideas are hardly likely to have contributed to the politician's electoral proposals in the first place. Such a situation may be in tune with the Burkean concept of Representation, but it certainly clashes with the purpose of Delegation, and it is the latter which really underpins democracy in directly connecting the voter with governmental intentions or the wishes of the electorate.

Many politicians, across the party political spectrum, will nowadays blithely declare that "class" no longer has any meaning in politics or society, and stubbornly maintain such an opinion, but as soon as an election is in sight, they surprisingly change their stance. It is then that the "Knockabout game" reintroduces the element of class into the electoral fight ahead. All these factors, and their deceit, disgust the majority of decent men and women who prefer to retain a disinterested view of proffered promises.

The root of the problem is traceable to the fact that democracy is dependent on issues that divide society in a real sense, and are not pretentious or invented as artificial grounds for difference or conflict. Such divisions are usually economic in modern or socially aware societies, but they may be cultural,

ADVANCING TECHNOLOGICAL CIVILISATION 63

religious, or racial, although these latter are usually unconscious or unknowing causes for underlying economic divisions. The left/right struggle that as a mechanism has successfully maintained democracy and pushed forward progress for some 200 years is now ineffective, outdated and falling apart due to several factors.

Firstly, there are no longer the grounds for a class conflict between Haves and Have-nots because legislation has created a society where egalitarianism is equally balanced against the demands for freedom. Secondly, there are no longer sufficiently large divides between differing economic interest groups to justify the practicable representation in maintaining the methodology for such democracy. Hence, the left/right divide has been reduced to the status of a pretentious struggle.

This is not to argue there are no longer economic divisions in society, but they are not class-based, and they are not and cannot be addressed by the existing economic system. The polarisation of society by our usurious and malign financial-industrial system works quietly – almost as an undercover movement – in destroying individual ownership, in both the domestic and business fields, through concentrating property in ever fewer hands. The increasing enrichment of the super-rich is not giving rise (or has not yet given rise) to a new and oppressed proletariat at the base of society, but it is disempowering the middle majority, day by day, in controlling the means of production and distribution.

As long as living standards or debt are not too adversely affected, discontent may not be widely expressed. It should, however, be noted that the banks and financial establishment are now tolerating levels of personal debt that would have been inconceivable in any earlier period of history. Why is this? Quite simply because the repayment of such personal debt within traditional time limits is currently impossible for the majority, and the exertion of undue pressure by the authorities would lead to the outbreak of protest on an intolerable scale. Public debt can always be removed through the banks' creation of money, but the millstone of personal debt never can.

Nonetheless, there are social pressures within society. The younger generation are not only oppressed by the need to repay student loans for further education that once was free; but are unable to get their foot on the bottom rung of the property ladder due to the hyper-inflation of values. Many remain with their parents until their 40s or even 50s, whilst many more cannot afford marriage or the gift of children, and hence the tragic collapse in the birth rate of those most skilled and educated in our technological civilisation. In turning to the retired, many discover that their Personal Pension plans fail to meet original estimates as they were based on the fallacy of equity investments. The selling of such plans was therefore based on a fraud.

Note should be taken of the causes for the hyper-inflation of property values. Again, the super-rich are solely to blame. It was once argued that the wealthy were an economic benefit to the community in that their presence caused wealth to trickle down the social scale. That may have been the situation a hundred or more years ago, when the wealthy built factories and created jobs, but that is no longer the case. Today, there is everywhere the tendency for the wealthy to cause inflation by passing down higher costs on all kinds of services and products, but it is the passive assets of land and property where such inflation has become most dramatic.

When the wealthy look to investing their assets within the UK or America, there is little to tempt them, as so much manufacturing has already been transferred to overseas locations. In view of the paucity of productivity, it is only natural to turn to the passive assets of land and property, for if these are held over a period of time, their value will increase through natural inflation in bringing a profitable return. The competitive rush by the super-rich and powerful corporations into the purchase of land and property, was an additional boost in promoting their value, and hence the inescapable consequence of hyper-inflation.

The result of this visually is perhaps most evident in central London along the banks of the Thames, where vast apartment blocks have appeared, housing the rich, whilst the original inhabitants of those areas are pushed to the outer and poorer suburbs. The less visual consequences, on the other hand, have appeared through the purchase of huge rural areas by corporations (often foreign) for specialised agricultural projects, whilst such inflation has brought chaos and ruin to the traditional ethnic farming class, and a dramatic drop in essential food production.

In view of these new forms of inequality and injustice creeping into our society, it may be asked as to why the left fail to exploit such a situation, which some might regard as an ideal opportunity for their regeneration. Such inequality is not class-based but rather generational from all sectors of the community. The reason that the situation is not seized upon by the left is that it fails to fit in with their cultural mindset. This is a subject on which I can write with some authority as an active member of the Labour party, both locally and nationally, attached to a number of groups for 14 years between 1994-2008, having joined under the logical but mistaken impression they would be intent on promoting home-based productivity.

Despite arguments on the need to increase British manufacturing, it was not only difficult to overcome an underlying anti-business ethos, but also a hatred (for the most part hidden) of what they considered the privileged class. Elderly middle-aged women, for example, were initially friendly in assuming I was some sort of academic, but as soon as they realised I had a business background, I received the cold shoulder. Working class people from an industrial background, however, had a different attitude, and on one occasion I was asked to stand as a Parliamentary candidate for a Midlands constituency, but disappointment occurred as soon as they were overruled by the Blairite elite with their own candidate. The Labour party is now predominantly a middle class party of public sector employees, with little interest in economic questions beyond those that raise their own salaries.

Furthermore, the Labour party has little interest in the perceived problems of the middle class, or those who have replaced them, as their particular eye is concentrated on those at the bottom of society who are helpless, oppressed, and poverty-stricken. The irony, of course, is that those at the bottom of society in the advanced industrial economies of the West are today everywhere assisted with regard to food, lodging, essential utilities, and free accommodation and keep in the event of Caring Home need. If oppression exists, it is found amongst the middle majority arising from the consequences of a usurious financial system, but the modern left have neither the understanding nor curiosity to uncover the obscure machinations of financial power. Their only attention is on redistribution, but they are unprepared to comprehend the technicalities for social wealth creation on which responsible redistribution is dependent.

This brings into view the left's approach to the concept of class. They would argue that their end view is the creation of an egalitarian or classless society, but this fails to explain the practical outcome of their political ideology. The Labour and other parties of the left have always based their ideals on class victory, i.e., the predominance of Working class values over those they see as oppressors. And this perspective of resentment still prevails in view of the fact that the modern left are middle rather than working class in composition.

The left are essentially dominated by the cultural concept of class, entailing a mindset of those who are part of and promote the interests of an underclass against money and business ownership. If the latter did not exist, neither would they, either culturally or organisationally.

In reality the left are not committed to a classless, or even an egalitarian society, but rather to a Working class society with all its cultural and political baggage. They are psychologically locked into such a mindset through their anti-business ethos, for there is no compromise between this and the dynamic needs of a business community. This argument is made clearer through elucidating the conditions for a truly desirable egalitarian society as argued in this book. The theoretically based, "freedom of opportunity," or belief in "meritocracy," is not sufficient to create an egalitarian society.

There needs to be the encouragement of upward mobility throughout every sector of society throughout the educational system from nursery level upwards. There can only be one standard of behaviour, manners, and culture, based on the upper-middle levels of society, for the inspiration of all the population, as otherwise there can be no realistic egalitarian system or even purpose. Table manners and style of speaking, in terms of both grammar and accent, should be taught as a standard acceptable in the highest circles. Otherwise, how else could those born in the poorest or most disadvantageous circumstances hope to freely associate with or rise with ease to the highest occupational or social levels?

This is egalitarianism balanced equally with freedom. It may be that, as yet, there are no such universal standards in existence as described above, because they have not had the time or opportunity to evolve within the new middle majority.

Hence, we are not arguing for the imitation of any particular high-class standards that may be perceived as existing at the present day. What we are advocating is something completely new with a specific constructive purpose.

Whilst none of the above conditions may exist in Britain or America, such cultural conditions covering class may be said to almost exist in their entirety in Germany, the Benelux and Scandinavian countries. The attitude of the Labour party, and the left generally, as noted in an earlier chapter, is to adopt the now fashionable *diversity* philosophy through positive discrimination policies, which are demeaning in their patronising attitude in assuming that such handicaps are necessary in the first place. Those exposed to such unearned gestures, must forever in their hearts, feel the humiliation of such experience. In addition, as also noted above, it devalues and debases educational standards in numberless ways. The standardisation of nurture and education towards a universal goal is the only true path to a democratic and just society. In this way, all are born, live, and die in equality of status – or as near to such a possibility.

If the above seems to convey a too-severe criticism of the left, it should be added that the right are as bad or worse, since their uncritical acceptance of Rentier capitalism has given rise to all the economic evils of our time – or, all such evils are traceable to the faults of the financial system. In view of such a situation, a fresh approach should be taken of socio-economic ills, that repudiate entirely a left/right perspective of society. Unless this question is resolved, the moral authority of our Technological Civilisation can never be justified in leading the world towards a better future. This is a topic to which we shall return in a later chapter.

CHAPTER 7
The Barriers to Free Thinking

"Those who fail to see that population growth and climate change are two sides of the same coin are either ignorant or hiding from the truth. These two huge environmental problems are inseparable and to discuss one while ignoring the other is irrational."

James Lovelock, *Population Reduction 'Max 1 Billion'*
& *Population Matters* website

The greatest barrier to progress at the present time is a society where the expression of new thinking is either blocked, or otherwise made impossible to exist through a variety of circumstances. This is a topic that needs to be seriously addressed if Technological Civilisation is to flourish for the longer term.

A superficial and popular explanation given for this situation is that in the Western world, living standards have reached a sufficient level in generating a universal complacency on the state of existence, and that hence there is little inducement to think beyond the day-to-day needs of the individual. This may be true, but such a situation may always have existed to some extent. But if true, there is no indication that the world is currently free from widespread threats that are actually, and not merely potentially, destroying life on our planet.

In America, whose people are amongst the most complacent of all, hundreds of forest fires have destroyed dozens of towns and villages in the West coast states of Washington, Oregon and California, resulting in the loss of homes for hundreds of thousands. The smoke and harmful carbon-dioxide from these uncontrolled fires, have not only crossed the continent from West to East, but crossed the Atlantic to create a red sky visible in Britain. It is apparent that these fires are of little concern to Americans beyond the three states affected. Their cause is due to several years of abnormal drought. Whilst "climate change" is denied, the official reason given for the fires is "poor forest management" and the "failure to clear away dead leaves."

The absurdity of these explanations, bordering on the comical, is enough to startle the most obtuse intelligence. And this is particularly so in view of other but equally destructive disasters in the southern and eastern states of America, through unprecedented and horrific storms and floods flattening everything in their path. An additional prompt to Americans that the forest fires in the Western states are climate-change induced, should be the reminder of even greater forest fires in the Yakutia area of north eastern Siberia, just below the Arctic circle, together with the accompanying underground peat fires beneath what for millennia had been permafrost.

The native inhabitants of the region have warned of previously unheard of heat during the summer months year by year. It takes a very complacent mindset to deny climate change in such circumstances. But denial, it must be admitted, is the easiest exit to anxiety, or the need to realise that something is seriously amiss.

In Britain, and elsewhere, it may be argued we are free to think, write, and act as we please, but such theoretical or practical rights are not sufficient in defining the free society. Freedom *from* wrongs and oppression are easily comprehended, as they immediately hurt the senses, and are attended to by demanded legislation. But freedom *for* a greater consciousness of the implications of our changing environment or the need for the fuller development of our potential, are things that need to be learned or taught. Unless these are developed, our freedom is no better than that of the ordinary cat or dog that reacts to instinctive emotion alone.

The reason for the need of the latter is that we are all subject to power or authority of which we may be unaware, or may be contrary to our interests. This is more so in complex or sophisticated societies, where power tends to be increasingly hidden from the rising educational standards and abilities of the majority. Power or authority can only exert its control through secretly buying off, or somehow rewarding, those whom it wishes to influence. The Roman satirist, Juvenal, was the first to use the term, *panem et circuses* (bread and circuses), in describing this process in securing the loyalty of the people to accept conditions that were not necessarily to their best advantage.

At the present time it is said we have a free press, although few now believe in the reality of this, after a long succession of powerful moguls from Harmsworth, Beaverbrook, Thomson, the Barclay brothers, Rothermere, Maxwell, Murdoch, etc., who have taken over, dominated, and destroyed administrations in their time, whilst wielding huge financial control from a discreet distance. If the above operated in Britain, other lists could be made of equally powerful press moguls who similarly flourished in other countries.

If their direct influence on government could not be hidden from public view, the presentation style of their newspapers and magazines nonetheless falsely conveyed an open impression of free speech whilst also implementing a policy of censorship surrounding a number of issues. The most deplorable aspect of many British newspapers and magazines is that they only publish articles by their own appointed circle of journalists, who may either be employees or freelancers, and in this way a clever control is ensured over both subject matter and opinion. These contributors have their favourite themes, to which they return again and again, and so regurgitate ideas that are already within the public domain, and are accepted unthinkingly by the readership.

There is nothing adverse in this in itself, as it anticipates readers' expectations and ensures the popularity of the media concerned. What does expose the press to justifiable criticism, however, is that no allowance is made for the expression of new ideas, or for real depth to be given to the discussion of any topic. It may be that editors feel justified in refraining to publish anything that may be "above the heads" of their readers, or anything that may offend as being too controversial. It may also be that the greatest fear of all editors, in an age when print sales are contracting fast, is the publication of anything which for any reason might reduce circulation figures.

Irrespective of what any editor may have in regard to the idea of a free press, the latter fails completely to promote the best interests of society defined as the necessary expression of freedom in its broadest approach. Such freedom needs to entail the expression of new and valued ideas, or the bringing into existence new knowledge, irrespective of whether it is wished-for or not by the public. This may be a demanding expectation, but in a world with accelerating rather than diminishing problems, it is a need that must be fulfilled if life on our planet is to survive.

Another and very significant reason explaining the non-existence of free or new thinking at the present time, is the consequence of total disillusion with contemporary politics. The low opinion in which politicians are now held, together with the meaninglessness of the left/right conflict, and the hypocrisy, pretension, and deceit that has filled the vacuum, has engendered a feeling of futility in regard to any discussion or attempt to develop new thinking. It is pretentiousness that has done much to undermine politics, for if on one day class struggle is acknowledged as "nonsense" and on the next, with the prospect of an election, it is regenerated, then how can an intelligent or honest discussion be possible with such a hypocritical turncoat? When can such a person be trusted to say what he really means?

The entire political environment of parliamentary politics is so suffused with deceit, that serious men and women choose to give it a wide berth and entrust the discussion of their ideas in any other circle – their home, their workplace, or the pub, but never to the slippery representative of their own constituency. The fact that real problems are now pushed under the carpet as inconsistent with traditional ideology, as described above, is another reason for the irrelevance of our politicians in addressing current issues.

One of the most significant barriers against free or creative thinking is derived from the increasingly corrupt influence of populist entertainment, usually through the broadcasting media. The ideals of John Reith that the media should act as a "public service to educate, inform and entertain," is fast disappearing. In the 1950s, both radio and television maintained high standards of integrity and culture, in producing classical plays by thought-provoking authors such as Ibsen, Chekhov, Shaw and Strindberg – names that are now unknown by the younger generation. It is true that Shakespeare is still presented, but in such appalling and eccentric productions that undermine the theme of the author in portraying the twisted perversions of one producer after another. For example, gender changes are made for leading characters, or else absurd attempts are made to identify the story with contemporary events in creating an anachronistic impression, or that otherwise distorts the author's purpose.

Worse still is sensationalism for its own sake or to achieve a questionable social perspective. Perhaps broadcasting achieved a unique low with a series of TV programmes suggesting that partners should be chosen through the sight of their genitals. This entailed groups of young men and women whose genitals were portrayed in close-up in choosing partners before the rest of their bodies were exposed to view. In other words, it was suggested that the shape, size, or beauty of their genitals was a better guide to developing a relationship than face to face communication. If that is to mark the future direction of society, then what hope for the better future of humankind?

If a social purpose can be derived from populist or demeaning entertainment, it can only be to undermine the capacity for free or creative thinking. It attempts and succeeds in achieving this through the crudest sensibility in arousing emotion of one kind or another, usually through violence or sexual titillation. It seeks to appeal to the lowest common denominator, i.e., to the least educated or most dull-witted intelligence. Although in America the broadcasting media may be worse than in Britain, it has in equal measure undermined the sagacity and acumen of her people in demeaning the potential good of humanity.

Who are the powers that be that help promote such a cultural environment, and what motivates them towards such an end? Broadcasting entertainment is dependent on high finance because of the huge cost entailed in maintaining a national network. The financial system has its own powerful and secret agenda, as we shall reveal in the following chapter, and its first purpose is to ward off questioning or discussion of its real role in influencing society. The best way in achieving this is to detract the populace from serious thinking about any public issues, and the easiest way is to focus the attention of the majority on the opium of light entertainment through violence and sex.

We return here to the topic of "bread and circuses," but the medium of television is far more subtle and effective than the killing of animals, or gladiators of each other in the Roman amphitheatre. The promoters and producers of television programmes, however, would give a different interpretation. They would argue the need for popularity in preventing falling viewing figures, and to achieve this, it is necessary to concentrate on those they categorise (or imagine) are at the lower end of society. With this in mind, they intentionally avoid what they describe as a "middle class bias," in the realisation that for decades in the past broadcasting was dominated by a middle class emphasis.

Hence, all this needed to change in the name of "greater democracy" in fulfilling the new concept of *diversity*. The greater reality, of course, is that "greater democracy" is not achieved through such a course, for a host of reasons in holding back the development of a better society. The new reality of the newly emerging middle majority is not yet recognised by the broadcasting media, whilst their concept of those at the *lower end of society* is not only insulting, but an idea plucked out of the sky. The broadcasting media still accept the traditional ideological view of a left/right split in society, and in response, they promote the latest left of centre ideas on diversity. But in actuality diversity creates a greater divide in society, rather than the contrary, as we have shown in an earlier chapter, and so the broadcasting media have been grossly misled by following outdated political ideology.

Another issue that needs to be addressed in undermining the promotion of free thought, is the rise of the Youth culture, most specifically in the sphere of popular music. The youth culture first emerged in America through the influence of foreign minority groups, and was soon seized upon by unprincipled financial interests perceiving a new and easy source of profit. The call for a youth culture was both unique and unnecessary. It was unnecessary in assuming that young people were incapable of appreciating a higher standard of music, or classical music, or that appealing to adults.

Of course there had always existed what may be described as "popular music," but this had an equal appeal to all age groups. Light music was either derived from folk, dance or military traditions, or derived from other tuneful or popular melodies. The youth culture, on the other hand, gave rise to music encouraging separation from the adult world, and a form of infantilism, and far worse, to the culture of drug-taking and drug addiction, which has remained until the present day. Until the rise of the youth culture, a popular drug culture had never existed.

This is not to suggest that drug addiction was unknown in earlier periods of history, for in 19th century Europe, it was probably more widespread than at present. But in earlier periods, drug addiction usually arose through the misuse of pain-avoiding medication, until legislation towards the end of the 19th century banned the sale of dangerous substances. If there ever existed what may be called a "drug culture," it only appeared in the occasional writings of such rare individuals as Coleridge or De Quincey.

The youth culture never penetrated Europe until the later 1940s, with the arrival of Rock'Roll, and similar forms of music, when it was widely accepted by the proletariat but disdained and rejected by the educated majority. I well remember at the time that my school contemporaries were universal in condemning such music as both depraved and ridiculous. Some years later, I learned that German friends had even been reprimanded by parents for "disgracing German civilisation," by surreptitiously listening to "degenerate" American music on the radio. Irrespective of the opinion we might now hold of the screeching sounds of the youth movement, the so-called "culture" must be condemned as a social evil, not only on account of its inseparable connection with drug addiction, but because it hinders adult development, and in every way creates a mindset in discouraging a thoughtful temperament or even the capacity for intelligence.

In Britain, over the decades, the broadcasting media have devalued the standards of the English language in several ways: not only through ungrammatical speech or the sloppy use of expressions, but through the presentation of the spoken word. In this context, complaints over the inability of actors in popular dramas have long been widespread. Young actors are no longer taught to "throw" their voices as from a stage, but are now dependent on microphones beneath their chins – even in the theatre. Meanwhile, their gabble on TV is further smothered by background music now regarded as an essential accompaniment in creating atmosphere.

In regard to sloppy talk, the word "them" is often used when "those" is intended (or should be), whilst "less" is used for things that are countable instead of the more accurate "few," and "challenged" is used as a universal word for anything that might be described as "difficult." On the day when writing these lines, I heard a BBC News presenter use the word "irreconcilable" when his intended meaning was clearly "irresolvable." Meanwhile, the word "of" is often used when the correct preposition is "with." The lack of any standard for pronunciation naturally contributes to difficulty of understanding. This is not to criticise the use of regional accents, but clarity of speech should always prevail. If one tunes into the repeat programmes made in the 1950s or early 60s, one is immediately struck by the crystal clarity and even beauty of the spoken English language when high standards of classical speech were still upheld.

The broadcasting media are much to blame for devaluing and corrupting the language, but they have followed this course in the pursuit of "proletarianization" or what they would falsely describe as the "democratisation" of society. In corrupting the language they also undermine the ability for its use in *expressing* reason or the accuracy necessary for intelligent discussion on any topic. In schools at the present time, grammar is no longer systematically taught as a subject in its own right, and so consequently the language is badly misused. Fowler's *Modern English Usage* should once again be made a subject for compulsory study throughout the school system.

If the media's intention is to create an egalitarian society – which it probably is – then such egalitarianism aims at the lowest educational level, and such a society would be incapable of maintaining an advanced Technological Civilisation deserving its name. The conditions contributing to a truly desirable egalitarianism have been amply described in earlier chapters. If the use of the English language is to regress at the rate it has over the past 60 years, it will eventually be reduced to a series of grunts with no more meaning than those of a chimpanzee.

The most serious barriers to free thinking must surely stem from the current situation of academia. The problem may be divided between structural and philosophical approaches. The structural problem has arisen from the huge accumulation of information in all spheres of knowledge at the present time, and the difficulty for its organisation and management for study and research. The consequence is that knowledge is divided into ever-more specialisms that are locked into their own exclusive departments tending to hinder inter-disciplinary studies. This means that academics are learning more and more about less and less. In the real sciences, such as medicine, dentistry, physics, chemistry, or mathematics, the problem is far less, as such subjects can only be properly comprehended and discussed through an inter-disciplinary approach towards progress along a practical and logical path.

But in the pseudo-sciences, such as economics, or those covering socio-political topics, a different situation pertains. This is because they depend so heavily on theory or opinion rather than facts, and so every academic locks him- or herself into a narrow knowledge box, where specialisms are fought for as life or death issues. Academics are forced to maintain their hard-fought for reputations, in jealously guarding their preserves against interlopers who are always a threat. At the same time, they refrain from intruding on another's territory, and in this way a tense harmony is maintained – at least for a period of time.

The academic's situation is also made vulnerable through the anonymous system of peer review, whereby research papers may only eventually see the light of day through publication in appropriate journals. In this way researchers are intimidated and confined within restricted limits. It also adds to the mutual suspicion and mistrust amongst academics involved in related specialisms. Personal experience over a number of years, in discussing a wide variety of socio-economic issues with leading academics, has amply confirmed the above allegations. Often they took place in small rooms along the many corridors of the LSE. There always came a point during such discussions when a query could not be answered and I was advised to consult so-and-so down the corridor

Two things struck me as particularly significant during these meetings: firstly, the paucity of general knowledge on the topic of the person consulted; and secondly, the viciously cat-like hostility amongst such academics – and like cats, each stood separately apart. The entire intellectual environment in which they worked, seemed opposed to a constructive attitude necessary in creating new knowledge. Hence, it is no wonder that nonsense is made of many claims to "scientific finality" in economics and other social sciences, when such specialists are grabbed and used by conflicting political groups in pursuit of their questionable ends. The claim that inter-disciplinary knowledge may override such barriers has not been borne out in actuality.

The problem of the philosophical approach of contemporary academics to knowledge is even more threatening to the cause of democratic progress than the structural problem, as it is far more deeply rooted. The practical approach to thinking with its suspicion of theory has a long tradition in Britain, and it was only after a period of many years that the work of our greatest philosopher, David Hume, was taken up for serious study – even though his empirical outlook in addressing problems was already well-established at the time. It is not sufficiently appreciated that theory, or the creation of *ideas*, is invariably the first step to any practical action or invention, or change of any kind. Whilst critical ideas are always necessary in stemming faulty thinking or ills of any kind, it is only through constructive ideas that progress is pushed ahead.

We now live in an age when constructive thinking is under perpetual attack by academia on a worldwide scale. As soon as any proposition is made, it is met by a negative response which goes on to assert that nothing is provable, and that nothing can be subjected to a measurement of value. In this way, the mouths of our academics are sealed, and thinking is blocked. Whilst in the normality of the outside world every conceivable topic may continue to be discussed in homes, workplaces, and pubs, those supposedly amongst the most professionally knowledgeable of our population are stopped in regard to the expression of constructive thinking for fear of being set-upon by their peers.

This is because at the core of our 21st century intellectual environment is the poison of postmodernism, which having linked-up with cultural Marxism with its Marcusian intolerance of tolerance, as a worldwide academic influence, is undermining the rationality of constructive thought that has dominated philosophy for 2,500 years until early in the 20th century. In addition, is its repudiation of the concept of the comparison of value, so that nothing may be considered as better than another. The roots of postmodernism may be traceable to a valid approach in resolving scientific or artistic issues at the start of the 20th century, but when carried over and mistakenly applied to the social sciences, it destroyed common sense and undermined effective analysis.

It is disgraceful and absurd that whilst free and informed discussion may still be pursued amongst the lay population, as soon as it is embarked upon by the power-wielding establishment, with its doctrinaire postmodernist principles, argument is stopped in its tracks along every step of the way. And that is why there is poverty of thought at the present time amongst the ruling elites, and why major political problems remain unresolved. Postmodernism may be described as the intellectual sickness of our age. The most common targets for its criticism over recent decades have included universalist ideas, objective reality, morality, truth, human nature, reason, science, language, and even social progress. Its thought is broadly characterised by tendencies to self-consciousness, self-referentiality, epistemological and moral relativism, pluralism and irreverence.

This is not to suggest that postmodernism has not been under intense attack since the time of its inception. Noam Chomsky has argued that it is meaningless because it adds nothing to analytical or empirical knowledge.[1] Camille Paglia has written that, "the art world will never revive until postmodernism fades away. Postmodernism is a plague upon the mind and heart."[2] Roger Scruton has asserted that, "a writer who says there are no truths, or that all truth is 'merely relative,' is asking you not to believe him. So don't."[3] The Christian philosopher, William Lane Craig, has said that, "The idea that we live in a postmodern culture is a myth. In fact, a postmodern culture is an impossibility. It would be utterly unliveable. People are not relativistic when it comes to matters of science, engineering, and technology."[4]

If the quality of academia has disintegrated amongst its leading proponents at the top of the profession, it has also encountered impediments at the lower levels amongst the student fraternity, usually under the leadership of student unions, through the sudden emergence of the intolerance of tolerance. On the spurious grounds of "protecting young minds" from offence, all kinds of absurd objections have been raised against the long-established descriptive labels of minority groups, together with hyper-sensitivity against critical opinions of many kinds. Not only are great numbers of students frightened against free expression by a minority of tyrannizing student leaders, but prominent lecturers have been barred from addressing public meetings for opinions judged as objectionable.

By this means an effective censorship has emerged in enforcing its authority throughout the world of further

---

[1] On Post-Modernism, Bactra.org website.
[2] "Postmodernism is a plague on the mind and the heart," in *Fausta Magazine*, 12th December 2015.
[3] Roger Scruton, *Modern Philosophy: an introduction and survey,* 1994.
[4] "God is not dead yet," in *Christianity Today*, 30th April 2014.

education. If, in fact, an academic has outraged the general public with the use of clearly offensive language about a particular race, as recently occurred with an eminent historian and TV presenter, then he should be prosecuted, and if found guilty, fined and possibly imprisoned, but on completing his sentence, he should then be allowed to return to his profession together with the right to free speech. This is because freedom of expression for all is an inalienable right without which democracy is no better than a sham. Those who prattle on about "offending young minds," or call for the silencing of others, are clearly enemies of free thought as well as free expression.

Closely connected with this is the movement to pull down statues, or otherwise attempt to remove the memory of the existence of those alleged to be associated with slavery. The extremism of these young people has even gone so far as to besmirch the reputation of historically heroic figures, including Gandhi, Sir Winston Churchill, and Vice-Admiral Nelson. It is not even suggested that such established people actually promoted slavery, but that in some obscure way were inadvertently, momentarily, or even unknowingly associated with its existence. It should also be borne in mind that Britain was the first country to take effective steps against slavery, and its success in this field should not only be remembered but celebrated with pride.

Apart from slandering the reputation of good people, it also introduces the question of applying 21st century values to those of earlier periods of history. Moral values evolve in the same way as technology, and it is anachronistic and nonsensical to apply those of the present time with those of the 18th or 19th century, or earlier, with their own distinctive ideals and purposes in life so different from our own. If those people who pull down statues or desecrate them with graffiti do not hate their own country and its history, they certainly convey the impression of doing so.

All the above paragraphs on the current difficulties of academia have seriously contributed to undermining the quality of university education on a worldwide basis. This is not to suggest that the highest qualities of teaching and research are still not maintained in the better and more exclusive centres of learning, but possibly 90% of such centres have been devalued below acceptable standards. Sixty or more years ago, a university education produced graduates with a broad and valued cultural knowledge. Today, that is no longer the case. Contemporary graduates may be competent in their studied specialisms but ignorant of everything else, and seldom able to convince others of their breadth of learning.

Having covered the leading, but by no means all, the barriers to free and creative thought at the present time,[5] we can now turn to the question of political censorship in contemporary Britain. It may be thought by the readers of this chapter, that as the conditions for free thought have been sufficiently undermined, then there would be no need for censorship. But there are still people in this country striving to convey a point of view that they regard as urgent and important, and there are others nonetheless equally determined to suppress their message. To this topic we shall now turn.

---

[5] Readers interested in a broader consideration of this topic may turn to the 12 chapters comprising Part IV entitled, *The Road to Constructive Politics*, of my book, **Egalitarianism of the Free Society** *and the end of class conflict*.

CHAPTER 8
Political Censorship in Contemporary Britain

"We need to recognise that slowing population growth is one of the most cost-effective and reliable ways of easing pressure on our environment and securing a sustainable future for us all."

Lionel Shriver, *Big Think Interview* & *Population Matters* website

I have always thought that those who suggest the existence of censorship in modern Britain must to some degree be victims of paranoia, and I have retained this lingering impression even after clear evidence to the contrary. Why is this? Britain has the worldwide reputation of being the founder of modern democracy, and moreover, is prepared nationally and internationally to fight and die for the cause. We feel safe on our streets and safe in our beds during the dark hours, and law-abiding citizens need never fear arbitrary arrest, or unwarranted surveillance, or cross-examination by unknown authorities.

But power in society, or pressure on the individual, need not solely originate from the state, or administration, or other legally recognised authorities. Government and its departments, and law in general, are not the only sources of power in society. Government is not absolute – and never has been – and may itself be under the power of forces of which it may be either aware or unaware. Whilst in olden times the Crown may have been under the power of the Church or the military, that is no longer the case.

Today, government is far more likely to be under the influence, or even within the grip of financial forces of which it is only half aware. But just as medieval kings would have repudiated the idea they retained their crowns on the sufferance of the Church or nobility, so contemporary governments likewise repudiate the idea that an intervening agency controls their actions. Governments, both medieval and modern, must maintain an appearance in the eyes of their people that they exert direct authority that is little short of absolute, as how else could they ensure the loyalty that comes from strength? It may be that governments are self-deceived, but that comes from double-think and the guile they are forced to use.

A concrete example may be cited: in 1997, a Labour government was elected, with cheers and banners flying, after many years of Tory rule. It was announced that a new political era had begun, and no one, Tory, Labour or Liberal doubted that fact. It was not until many years later, following the next Tory victory, that commentators made public and discovered the fact, that both Tony Blair and Gordon Brown, as premiers, had continued the pursuit of Thatcherite economic policies, even though both had condemned the same throughout the duration of their office. Surprisingly, nothing had changed! It was already well-known they had cultivated friendships with powerful press tycoons who had assisted them in their election campaigns, but little more was thought of the matter, as nothing contrary could be achieved. When Gordon Brown entered Number 10, one of his first actions was to invite in Margaret Thatcher for a friendly chat. At the time, no significance was given to the episode, and it was dismissed as an eccentricity.

Although the question may be asked as to what extent any government is controlled by external or democratically unaccountable forces, it is impossible to give an answer. This is because one cannot definitively assess as to whether the decisions of a premier or government are those of the latter, or those of an outside source, or those of a mind that may be changed at any time through good or bad motives. As one cannot read a man's (or a woman's) heart, it is impossible to know the truth of such a situation. In hazarding a guess, the worst conclusions are more likely to be the correct revelation of the truth. In the light of such a situation, most of us choose to stoically accept the world as it is, as there is little else we can do.

And this remains so even when confronting the problem of political censorship in contemporary Britain. And such censorship is unlikely to originate from government authority, except in the event of applying the Official Secrets Act of 1911, that was originally introduced to counter Imperial German espionage activity at the time. Since that period, however, in practice that Act has been extended to include the revelation by Civil Servants, or others, of any information regarding the work of their departments. For this reason, it has often aroused considerable controversy and opposition, not only because it has allegedly been applied to situations never intended at the time of its inception, but because it has led to a greater prohibition of knowledge as to the business of government than in any other country with a comparable reputation for democracy. The administrative system has become notorious for the secrecy in which it operates throughout Western Europe. This, therefore, is no encouragement to those who wish for a more open government, or to those who would wish to believe that political censorship of some kind was inconceivable.

As ultimate power cannot be guaranteed to arise wholly from that of government independent of external influences, but is more often the outcome of a mix of forces from varying directions, all censorship must ultimately be cast back as the responsibility of government for blame. All censorship is wrong, since it tramples on the freedom of people, except for that with the bona fide intention of safeguarding the security of the State. But even the latter is subject to varying definitions, and as we have seen above, a law that was intended to protect the country in a war-threatening situation, is now interpreted to protect our civil servants, or their departments, from any impropriety or wrongdoing.

The censorship that we are now opening for discussion concerns that of the financial-industrial system which is of direct interest to every citizen of this country, because of the many ways in which it impacts on our material welfare. It may even be argued that the financial-industrial system exerts a greater influence on our lives than the work of any elected government. Governments come and go according to a variety of popular or unpopular measures of a relatively superficial nature, whilst the financial-industrial system progresses like a steamroller along its own chosen path. It is now maintained that that system is political because of the breadth of its power, and the fact that it is democratically unaccountable – even untouchable – is irrelevant to that fact. Of course, it should by right be democratically accountable, but it is not.

Up to this point, readers may still remain unconvinced of the seriousness of political censorship in contemporary Britain, and I must admit that for a long period, even after experiencing its existence, I was reluctant to realise the extent of its evil - possibly through a mixture of fatalism and stoicism. I shall now recount my own confrontation with censorship, and then that I was to eventually witness elsewhere, and by the end of this chapter I anticipate that few readers will question the seriousness of the topic and the need for intervention.

It was in summer 1985 that I published my first pamphlet, *New Life for British Industry*, financed by the eminent industrialist, George Goyder, and it was in this work that the stark differences between Rentier and Productive capitalism were publicised for the first time. It was not until six years later that the French economist and financier, Michel Albert, produced a similar argument in his book *Capitalisme contre Capitalisme*. In November 1985 I lined up with George T, Edwards, a senior executive in the Post Office, who together with J.C. Carrington, had already written two important books, published by Macmillan, *Financing Industrial Development* (1979) and, *Reversing Industrial Decline* (1981). Both had formerly been students together at Edinburgh University, where they had been appalled at uncovering the corruption and destructive usury of the British financial institutions, and consequently set about to expose the scandal through their writings.

It was through my early contact with Edwards that I first came into contact with what I wrongly assumed was "paranoia." For eight years, as a Tory party member, he had sat on various sub-committees in promoting the cause of home-based productivity, most notably those connected with the activities of Sir William Grylls, but his efforts were in vain. On the publication of the second book cited above, he and Carrington were approached by a group of businessmen and congratulated on their intelligence and percipience, and offered top-salary posts on a life-time basis with worldwide travel, if they would keep their mouths shut and renege on their beliefs. Both men refused the offers made.

The group then returned with threats to ensure their dismissal from their current employment if they wrote another word on the issues raised. Carrington, who worked for British Telecom, never put pen to paper again, and continued to enjoy a progressive career in that company. Edwards, on the other hand, produced two more books published by Macmillan, *How Economic Growth and Inflation Happen* (1984), and, *The Role of the Banks in Economic Development* (1988). In the mid-80s he was seconded by the Post Office to work for another organisation, supposedly on a temporary basis, but never returned to his former employment. Hence, the ultimate threat had been carried out.

On 6th August 1987, Edwards and I initiated the founding meeting of the Campaign for Industry (CFI) in the City office of Unity Trust in Carlisle Avenue, hosted by its director, Terry B. Thomas, who subsequently became the Chairman of the Cooperative Bank. Also present at that meeting was Lord Gregson of Stockport (elected President of the CFI), Dr. A.B. Gozzard, Group Personnel Director of Plessey, Dr. John Hart, a scientist turned businessman, and a professor from a well-known business school, who shall remain nameless for reasons cited below. Not attending the meeting but also elected onto the board with their authority were John Carrington (who felt he need not compromise his earlier undertaking), Keith Smith, a lecturer at Keele University and author of *The British Economic Crisis*, and Prof. Sidney Pollard, the most eminent economic historian of 20th century Britain, whom I had visited in Bielefeld the previous summer, where he had been seconded from Sheffield University. Edwards and I were respectively elected Vice-Chairman and Chairman of the association.

After the meeting, Edwards, John Hart, and I, adjourned to a nearby pub where we discussed the future of the CFI. I was soon struck again by what I assumed was Edwards' "paranoia" when he exclaimed, "I wonder who will turn out to be "the spy" amongst the group. At first, all seemed to go smoothly, but suddenly, after a couple of months, the following offered their immediate resignation within a 3-week period for differing reasons: T.B. Thomas, Lord Gregson, Dr. Gozzard, and the professor from the business school. It could not have been a coincidence that all four resigned within so short a time period, but it was the letter from the professor that assured me that foul play must have played a part.

The letter consisted of a furious tirade in which the writer claimed he had "never" supported the movement, had "never" attended the said meeting, and that his name should immediately be withdrawn from our letterheads. The fury of the letter made no sense. There were six witnesses to the fact that the said academic had not only attended the meeting, but that he had fully participated in electing other members, and in endorsing the constitution and other decisions that had been made. How then could he possibly write a letter of such stupidity? The explanation could only be that he had been severely threatened and frightened out of his wits. This is a concrete example of the ruthless methods employed by financial interests in suppressing freedom of speech. It is also an example of political censorship carried to its successful conclusion. As the CFI was deprived of funds, apart from those of the present author, it was restricted to the sphere of merely producing socio-economic pamphlets from time to time.

This was an unsatisfactory way ahead, for although continued research helped to produce new arguments and strengthen old, only organisational action in cooperation with others could hope to effect change. But as those who are little known, or of limited resources, or otherwise unable to win attention, are helpless; there is little point in feelings of anger or resentment, or even in harbouring the emotion of disappointment. But eventually, after many years, another event occurred, which seemed to cast the situation in quite another light.

On the morning of Wednesday 18th September 2019, I was startled by the publication of what I took to be an extraordinary issue of the *Financial Times*. On that day, this world-leading financial newspaper, launched what it described as *The New Agenda*. In arousing special attention, the paper appeared in a yellow wrapper, on the front of which was written:

"*Capitalism. Time for a Reset.* Business should make a profit but should serve a purpose too."

Its leading feature, written by the Economics Editor, Martin Wolf, was headed: "*Saving Capitalism from the Rentiers* a dynamic economy gives everybody the belief they may share in the benefits. Instead, weak competition, feeble productivity growth, high inequality and a degraded democracy are failing citizens." The full page article, supported by statistical tables, not only repeated all the arguments I had presented over a 40-year period, but even used my terminology. The following are two examples of sub-headings appearing in the article: "Rentier capitalism means an economy in which privileged individuals and business extract a great deal of rent from everybody else," and, "Companies benefit from the public goods provided by most liberal countries, yet they are also in a perfect position to exploit tax loopholes."

Inside the front cover of the paper, in large print, under the heading, *Introducing the New Agenda*, was published the following letter by its Editor, Lionel Barber:-

Dear Reader.

The *Financial Times* believes in free enterprise capitalism. It is the foundation for the creation of wealth which provides jobs, more money and more taxes.

The liberal capitalist model has delivered peace, prosperity and technological progress for the past 50 years, dramatically reducing poverty and raising living standards throughout the world.

But in the decade since the global financial crisis, the model has come under strain, particularly the focus on maximising profits and shareholder value. These principles of good business are necessary but not sufficient.

The long-term health of free enterprise capitalism will depend on delivering profit with purpose. Companies will come to understand that this combination serves their self-interest as well as their customers and employees. Without change, the prescription risks being far more painful.

Free enterprise capitalism has shown a remarkable capacity to renew itself. At times, as the historian Thomas Babington Macaulay wisely noted, it is necessary to reform in order to preserve. Today the world has reached that moment. It is time for a Reset.

In the same newspaper, on the Opinion page, appeared an excellent article by the eminent American lawyer, well-versed in business matters, Martin Lipton, headed, *Directors have a duty to look beyond their shareholders.*

On the back page of the yellow wrapper appeared the following statements in bold print capitals:-

WE LIVE IN A TIME OF DISRUPTION AND FRAGMENTATION BUT WHERE OTHERS SEE DIFFICULTY, WE SEE OPPORTUNITY – NOT JUST TO SURVIVE BUT TO THRIVE

TO STAND UP FOR WEALTH CREATION AND FREE ENTERPRISE AS DRIVERS OF DEVELOPMENT

TO PROMOTE BETTER BUSINESS BY HOLDING COMPANIES TO ACCOUNT

TO EMPOWER EACH OTHER TO LEAD THE WAY IN BUSINESS, SOCIETY AND THE WIDER WORLD

THIS IS THE NEW AGENDA

This remarkable issue of the *Financial Times* attracted sufficient attention to be noted on Radio 4's *Today* programme, as well as by the author of this book, who was keen to follow the eventual outcome of the New Agenda. After several days of silence, I felt it necessary to enquire into any progress that might have been made. I spoke with Martin Wolf, who explained that as the Economics Editor, he customarily worked alone without cooperation from others. I also spoke with Joshua Oliver, an assistant to Lionel Barber, who tentatively suggested that "progress would be made," but heard nothing thereafter.

In studying the contents of this particular issue of the paper, it might have been argued that the relevant authors had simply copied and reprinted passages from my own books – but this was certainly not the case. The contents of the paper, as well as those of my own writings, had merely recorded the factual and objective truth as it existed. The authorship of the contents was therefore of no more significance than the fact that two and two makes four.

By the end of the year, Lionel Barber was no longer Editor of the FT. Nothing more was ever heard of the *New Agenda*, and nothing appeared in print associated with the issue of 18th September. I was left with the impression that those with whom I spoke at the FT were scared by the consequences of an initiative that should never have been embarked upon. The project could never have been thought-up and implemented at a moment's notice. It must have been carefully planned in advance and costs were obviously entailed.

Teamwork must have been involved, and proper discussion before decisions were reached. All this would have culminated in a spirit of purpose and determination. How then could the project have been ditched at a moment's notice without explanation of any kind? It could only have come about through unpleasant threats from a very determined source. It must be assumed that the FT could never have anticipated such strength of opposition to their project as otherwise they would never have embarked upon it in the first place. It would indicate that the editorial policy of the paper is ultimately answerable to financial forces overriding any objective stance it chooses to adopt.

In the weeks that followed, I wrote an article on the episode and its significance in regard to censorship and the expression of free political opinion, and sent it to every quality national daily. The article was never published, and I never received an acknowledgement from any editor. We now live in an age when cowardice over the expression of free political opinion in Britain is greater than at any time in living memory. If it is not cowardice, it is a question of choice between permitting free opinion or safeguarding personal income.

There was a time when I was aghast at reading about those who had sacrificed their lives at the stake for the expression of free opinion or belief. Was it a waste of life or a justified decision? I am now convinced it was the latter. Progress, or the revelation of new knowledge – or the cause of civilisation – can only advance through the creation and expression of new ideas, but such conviction can only advance through the courage it demands.

I now realise that those who strove for the truth of the new have always welcomed the flames of the stake to the shameful alternative of living a lie. The evidence of history seems to be that their decisions were made with ease, free from the hesitation of doubt. For these reasons, and all that has been revealed in the past two chapters, our Technological Civilisation cannot hope to advance or maintain its moral leadership as the ultimate authority without the unity of peoples towards that end.

CHAPTER 9
The Environmental Threats to Planet Earth

"It's been so obvious to me for so long that cramming ever more people onto our little planet does ever more damage - I cannot understand why so many people find this so hard to grasp, and why so many governments ignore it."

Susan Hampshire, Video interview & *Population Matters* website

Before returning to the subject of the type of international organisation required in confronting the population question, it would first be apt to summarise the overall threat to the environment in regard to the need for population reduction. We are here considering the threat to the planet's ecosystem as something that should be prioritised over the threat to the human species, and this places the problem in a very special light in regard to ethical issues.

As humankind cannot survive without the health of the planet, which gave rise to the species in the first place, there would be little sense in reversing this order of priority. To do so, would be to reduce the level of the discussion to meaningless and futile sentimentality.

The interdependence of everything on the planet defines its totality as a living organism: glaciers and ice-sheets, rivers and forests, cloud-cover and mountains, no less than bees, birds, or ruminants – or even humans – as the first everywhere support the life of the latter. If the planet is now threatened then humankind is to blame, and only the latter can attempt to reverse the situation. Since the beginning of the industrial revolution, the acidity of surface ocean waters has increased by about 30%. This increase is the result of humans emitting more carbon-dioxide into the atmosphere and hence more being absorbed into the oceans. The amount of carbon-dioxide absorbed by the upper layer of the oceans is increasing by about 2 billion tons per year. When the addition of accelerating quantities of plastics are dumped in the sea, or flow inadvertently from sewers, rivers and streams, to enter the stomachs of fish and other creatures offering a food source for humans, the scale of death and destruction may be anticipated.

The heat-trapping nature of carbon-dioxide and other gases was demonstrated already in the 19th century. Their ability to affect the transfer of infrared energy through the atmosphere is the scientific basis of many instruments flown by NASA. There is no question that increased levels of greenhouse gases must cause the Earth to warm in response. The planet's average surface temperature has risen about 1.62 degrees Fahrenheit, or 0.9 degrees Celsius, since the 19th century, a change driven largely by increased carbon-dioxide and other human-made emissions into the atmosphere. Most of the warming has occurred in the past 35 years, with the 6 warmest years on record taking place since 2014. Not only was 2016 the warmest year on record, but eight of the 12 months that make up the year – from January through to September, with the exception of June – were the warmest on record for those respective months.

The current warming trend is of particular significance as approximately 95% of it has resulted from human activity since the mid-20th century, and is proceeding at a rate that is unprecedented over decades and millennia. Earth-orbiting satellites and other technological advances have enabled scientists to see the big picture, collecting many different types of information about our planet and its climate on a global scale. This body of data, collected over many years, reveals the signals of a changing climate. The oceans have absorbed much of this increased heat, with the top 700 metres, or 2,300 feet, of ocean showing warming of more than 0.4 degrees Fahrenheit since 1989.

Meanwhile, glaciers are retreating almost everywhere around the world, including in the Alps, Himalayas, Andies, Rockies, Alaska and Africa. The Greenland and Antarctic ice sheets have decreased in mass. Data from NASA's Gravity and Climate Experiment show Greenland lost an average of 286 billion tons of ice per year between 1993 and 2016, while Antarctica lost about 127 billion tons of ice per year during the same period. The rate of Antarctica ice mass loss has tripled in the last decade. Consequently, global sea level rose about 8 inches in the last century, but the rate over the last two decades was nearly double that of the previous century, and is accelerating every year.

Ice cores drawn from Greenland, Antarctica, and tropical mountain glaciers have clearly shown that the Earth's climate responds to changes in greenhouse gas levels. Ancient evidence can also be found in tree rings, ocean sediments, coral reefs, and layers of sedimentary rocks. This ancient, or paleoclimate evidence reveals that current warming is occurring roughly ten times faster than the average rate of ice-age-recovery warming. The melting of the Antarctic ice sheet will cause sea level rises of about two and a half metres around the world. The melting is likely to take place over an extended period, beyond the end of this century, but is almost certain to be irreversible because of the way in which the ice cap is likely to melt according to the latest models. Bearing this in mind, New York, London, and Shanghai will be amongst the leading cities to be inundated and made unliveable.

Even if temperatures were to fall again after rising by 2c (3.6 F), the ice would not recover its initial state because of self-reinforcing mechanisms that destabilises the ice. Anders

Levermann, co-author of the paper from the Potsdam Institute for Climate Impact Research, has maintained that, "The more we learn about Antarctica, the direr the predictions become. We get enormous sea level rise from Antarctica melting, even if we keep to the Paris Agreement, and catastrophic amounts if we don't." Twila Moon, a research scientist at the University of Colorado at Boulder, has said, "It's devastating to see yet another Arctic summer end with so little sea ice. Not only is there a very small area of sea ice, but it is also younger and more vulnerable overall. The Arctic is a changed place. All hope rests on humans to act on climate and slow this alarming pace of ice loss."

Antarctica's vast ice cap, which covers about as much of the Earth as North America is close to three miles (5 km) thick, holds more than half of the Earth's fresh water. Some of it is floating sea ice, which does not cause sea level rises in the way of ice melting from land, and is subject from above and below because of the warming sea. Researchers have examined how ice over land in the region can be expected to melt, and found a strong "hysteresis" effect, which makes it harder for ice to re-form than to melt. When the ice melts, its surface sinks lower down and sits in warmer air, so requiring lower temperatures for the ice to re-form than it did to keep the existing ice stable.

If temperatures rose by 4c above pre-industrial levels, which some argue is possible if the world fails to reduce greenhouse gas emissions soon, then the sea level rise would be 6.5 metres from the Antarctica alone, not counting the contribution from Greenland and other glaciers. That would be enough eventually to inundate all the world's coastal cities and cause devastation on a global scale.

The above facts, most recently revealed by leading scientists, might engender a spirit of total hopelessness. If that is the real situation, then why bother to address the problem?

That indeed may be the response of the majority of politicians worldwide together with a laziness to face any problem they feel is beyond their capability. And yet, if we believe that humankind should be spared from annihilation at any cost, then will-power applied to the best intelligence must be sought and pursued with vigour. The size and complexity of the problem is such that only new and untried ideas and practices should be considered. This is because old or long-established means would be doomed to failure if attempted to resolve an unprecedented threat to life on our planet.

Whilst the scientific problems of installing non-polluting energy sources as wind or tidal power, or solar panels, or the reform of agricultural systems, free of harmful fertilisers or pesticides, etc., on a global scale may be left to the ordinary procedures of scientists and government; the greater overall problem of population control and reduction must be promoted through a new type of political organisation. This is not to suggest that the population problem in recent years has not already been addressed by other individuals or organisations. The most notable writer on the topic was perhaps, Paul R. Ehrlich with his book, *The Population Bomb* (1968) that was updated many years later, in partnership with his wife, Anne Ehrlich, under the title, *The Population Explosion* (1990). Also, in 1968 appeared Garrett Harden's landmark essay, *Tragedy of the Commons*, in which he argued that society must relinquish the "freedom to breed" through "mutual coercion, mutually agreed upon." Later, in 1972, he reaffirmed his argument in a new essay, *Exploring New Ethics for Survival*, by stating, "We are breeding ourselves into oblivion."

In 2007, Jeffrey Sachs, head of the UN Millennium Project, delivered his series of Reith Lectures, *Bursting at the Seams*, in which he dealt with a number of problems associated with over-population and poverty reduction. Other prominent personalities who have advocated population planning are: Bertrand Russell and Margaret Sanger (1938), John D. Rockefeller and Frederick Osborn (1952), and Isaac Asimov, Arne Naess and Jacques Cousteau.

At the present time, the following well-known personalities and supporters of the movement Population Matters, may also be cited in this regard: David Attenborough; Chris Packham; Jane Goodall; Susan Hampshire; Sir Partha Dasgupta (Frank Ramsey Professor of Economics at the University of Cambridge); Sara Parkin; Sir Crispin Tickell (Director of the Policy Foresight Programme); and Prof. John Guillebaud (Emeritus Professor of Family Planning & Reproductive Health at University College, London). Other equally prominent names of individuals, or similar organisations, might be added to the above list, but space limits their inclusion.

Meanwhile, the Extinction Rebellion, founded by Roger Hallam and Gail Bradbrook, have courageously made an effective mark in arousing public concern, although their call for "disruptive civil disobedience" may be open to question if the response proves to be counter-productive. However, they are spot-on when they contend on their website that the "Conventional approaches of voting, lobbying, petitions and protest have failed because powerful political and economic interests prevent change."

They successfully emphasise the fact that, "We are facing an unprecedented global emergency. Life on Earth is in crisis: scientists agree we have entered a period of abrupt climate breakdown, and we are in the midst of a mass extinction of our own making. ... We have to move beyond the politics that have so far held us back."[6] The only surprise is that until the present time they have avoided the population issue. This is probably

---

[6] All quotes taken from the *Extinction Rebellion* website.

because their head-on abrasive approach would make it difficult to tackle the problem with the appropriate persuasive style for its ready acceptance.

Meanwhile, Greta Thunberg has made a remarkable impression on a worldwide scale in her unique way in arousing concern over the environmental crisis, as indeed has Charles, Prince of Wales, for decades past. When he first embarked on his campaign, before climate change was a topic of conversation, he was dismissed for his "eccentricity" and "sensationalism." He is now amongst the foremost heroes in the struggle to save the planet, and his son, William, Duke of Cambridge, is fast following in his father's footsteps. However, none of these three have yet attempted to tackle the population question effectively.

Despite the praiseworthy or determined striving of any of the above scientists or other notabilities, in the past or in the present, their combined efforts have not, as yet, succeeded in achieving their purpose. It is for this reason we shall now return to re-considering the main theme of this book.

CHAPTER 10
New Approaches to the Population Problem

"It's population growth that underlies just about every single one of the problems that we've inflicted on the planet."

Jane Goodall, Video: *Over-population in the Developing World*

Before re-considering the role of the proposed Tripartite Alliance, in underlying the urgency of the population problem, it would be useful to list some salient facts. At the present time the global population is increasing by 80 million a year.

Until the start of the 19th century there were less than 1 billion people on the planet. Since World War II, a billion people have been added to the population every 12-15 years, and the population has more than doubled since 1970. Every two years, the United Nations makes projections for future population growth, and its latest median projection is a population of 9.7 billion by 2050 and 10.9 by 2100. Because many factors affect population growth, it makes a range of projections depending on different assumptions. Within its 95% certainty range, the difference in population in 2100 from the highest to lowest projection is almost 4 billion people – more than half the population we have today.

By 2050, the following 9 countries will make up over half the projected total population increase: India, Nigeria, Pakistan, the Democratic Republic of the Congo, Ethiopia, Tanzania, Egypt, and the USA. Around 2027 it is expected that India will overtake China as the world's most populous country. Fifty-five countries are projected to experience a population reduction by 2050, and China's population is projected to decrease by 2.2% or 31.4 million. More than half of the people added to the world's population over the rest of the century will be in sub-Saharan Africa. Due to its high fertility rate, sub-Saharan Africa has a very young population: 60% being less than 25 years old. This means that huge numbers are now entering their childbearing years. Due to improvements in healthcare, life expectancy is increasing and child mortality is declining, which means there are more generations alive at the same time.

The uncontrolled human population increase brings into view the extinction of other animal species as a consequence of this. Since life appeared on Earth, there have been several mass extinctions in which many species were wiped out because of catastrophic climate change, volcanic activity, the impact of an asteroid, or other reasons not yet uncovered. The plants and animals which currently live on Earth have continued to evolve over 65 million years since the previous mass extinction. Many scientists consider the huge reduction in biodiversity since the emergence of humans is now on the scale of another mass extinction, and this would be known as the Anthropocene extinction – or the sixth mass extinction.

In illustrating this, it should be noted that the WWF's latest *Living Planet Report* estimates that we have already lost 60% of all vertebrate wildlife populations since 1970. That amounts to more than half of all birds, mammals, reptiles, amphibians and fish gone in just 50 years. During that time, our population has more than doubled, increasing from 3.7 billion to over 7.8 billion today. Invertebrates, while understudied, are not faring any better. A German study found that flying insect populations (including pollinators) have crashed by three-quarters since 1989, reflecting similar trends around the world.

In its landmark 2019 report, IPBES reported that one million species are now at risk of disappearing for good and according to the IUCN Red list of Threatened Species, 41% of amphibians, 25% of mammals, 34% of conifers, 13% of birds, 31% of sharks and rays, 33% of reef-building corals, and 27% of crustaceans are threatened with extinction. Some countries are worse off than others, and the 2016 *State of Nature* report concluded that the UK was one of the most nature-depleted countries in the world. Biodiversity loss is attributable to several causes, by far the biggest culprit are habitat destruction and over-exploitation of species, driven by our exploding numbers and unsustainable consumption.

The conventional approach to a crisis problem on such a scale would be to assemble all countries for an emergency conference – most probably under the auspices of the United Nations. Such an approach is now rejected on the grounds it would collapse under its own weight in a Miltonic pandemonium of anarchy where all were against all. This is because the *immediate* vested interests of the majority of peoples or nation states would prevail, and subjectively feel they were under attack. The final outcome, after the storm of such an episode, would be a great fatalism, and all would remain exactly as before. Although respect should be given to the many subsidiary or specialised departments of the UN, the central body (or General Assembly), has failed disastrously on so many occasions in confronting major issues, that it could not be depended upon in addressing the urgent problem now under discussion.

It is therefore imperative that the leading and most powerful industrially advanced economies, together with their best informed peoples unite, to assert their authority over the rest of the planet. But the assertion of such power is only practicable if based on moral authority that appeals to people worldwide, irrespective of their cultural or socio-economic status. However, it should be noted that financial or industrial power in itself, as currently found in the leading economies, has little or no appeal to the peoples of the wider world. This is because it is perceived, rightly or wrongly, as exploitative or self-serving for its own prosperity. Those who look closer at Western (or American) style capitalism, for example, soon perceive that the Rentier model is primarily concerned with maximising investors' profits at the cost of productivity or in fulfilling the needs of home-based economies, and worse still, is polarising wealth between the rich and less affluent.

The more perceptive and thoughtful peoples of the wider world laugh at the hypocrisy, or assume the hidden deceit of such leading industrial economies at any attempt to put themselves forward as the altruistic advance guard in saving the environment or confronting the population problem. That is why so great a part of this book has concentrated on questions of fairness as justice in the sphere of economics and politics.

Up to this point, we have centred such arguments on the criticism of the *as is* situation. We have condemned the Rentier system because of its self-destructiveness, and we have elucidated the bankruptcy of the left/right struggle as a democratic mechanism in further advancing the cause of progress. If both "privatisation" and left-inspired collectivism have failed as economic systems, and if democracy, as it currently exists, is breaking down and doomed to eventual extinction, what then?

We must naturally now turn to questions of reconstruction, so that these may be offered as benefits to the wider world in winning its inspiration and trust for the future role of the advanced industrial economies under the banner of Technological Civilisation. The purpose of its leadership would be to bring all peoples and nations within its orbit towards higher material standards, so that eventually a worldwide egalitarianism is achieved amongst all peoples and races.

This may be achieved through the promotion of the *Personalisation of Ownership* – something quite different from the deceptive term of "privatisation." If healthy democracy is to be regenerated for the future, it must be based on the interests of the *individual* in repudiating those collective values that siphon off authority into representative elites that in reality act according to their own changing volition rather than those of their electors. The personalisation of ownership is intent on granting direct as opposed to representative power to the individual wherever this is possible.

Whilst in the workplace this is achieved through co-determination and realistic means for employee share ownership (enabled through changes to Company law); in the political sphere, it is facilitated through systems of referenda on major or even lesser issues that arise. The personalisation of ownership is only practicable in those societies where an educated middle majority has emerged, where the will for management and ownership power is equally matched with skills and responsibility. It also entails the ideological repudiation of discredited left/right prejudices that divide rather than unite society. In this way, the shared management and ownership of business is maximised amongst all levels of employees in business enterprise to the financial benefit of all parties concerned, as well as contributing to the better efficiency of the same.

The question of changes to land management, both urban and rural, also comes under the heading of the personalisation of ownership. That the right to property stems from those who work it was already argued by John Locke 400 years ago. In Britain we find an almost unique situation in the advanced industrial economies, whereby the country is still divided into huge ownership territories inherited by a small number of aristocrats, or else purchased by super-rich individuals or organisations. These, in turn, lease or rent out the land, with the possibility of sub-letting on several levels. The effect of this is to inflate the sale value of all products from the land through such a monopolistic pattern of ownership.

In addition, much land held in this way in rural areas, is put to no good economic use, or to the wasteful use of sporting purposes that remove its greater potential value for agriculture or forestry. It is now argued that the huge rural territories revert to the Crown (through the agency of the State) through compulsory purchase from their owners (by way of compensation) over a 25-year period of annual instalments. Under the auspices of the National Farmers' Union, the land would then be divided into commercially viable plots for modern mixed or other farming purposes, or for profitable afforestation.

The same would then be sold under licence for their specific productive purpose, as inalienable hereditary properties, to suitably qualified families of good character, or to those selected to be trained for the desired skills. The NFU would supervise the management of such properties, and in the event of the extinction of a family line, would arrange for the re-sale of the property. Such arrangements would not only ensure the greater stability of the agricultural industry but increase its efficiency and profitability.

Of most dramatic significance would be the impact on widespread afforestation throughout Scotland and Wales, as well as in England. The greater part of the north of Britain (especially in the Highlands) could be under privately owned forestry plantations, but such families selected would necessarily be ethnic natives in their respective territories, in safeguarding the cultural integrity of their countries in the eyes of the rest of the population.

Meanwhile, the financial rationale of business should be directed by the principles of Productive as opposed to Rentier profitability. In this way, the proper role of business, which is *productivity* in best serving consumer needs, will be upheld. All employees throughout an enterprise should remain on guard against Rentier tendencies defined as wastage by any means, in addition to raised costs, howsoever made in diminishing the sales or marketing of the product or service entailed.

The greatest evil of Rentier capitalism, as noted in an earlier chapter, is the polarisation of wealth that is ultimately self-destructive to any kind of business. In such an environment, trades unionism would take on an extended role: rather than being primarily concerned with wages and conditions of employment, their main priority would be their vigilance against Rentier tendencies. Trades union leaders, as well as shop stewards, would therefore need to be qualified in accountancy, in fulfilling a role requiring sufficient knowledge and cautious in-depth judgement.

If the needs of employment-giving productivity are to be promoted, as well as the general economic interests of the majority population, these things cannot be achieved without the integrity of pursuing nationalist policies. The function of any honest government is to pursue the best interests of its own people as a first priority, and not those of transnational corporations or high finance, or "international interests" that are so often used as a cover by politicians to line their own pockets, or allow powerful bodies an easy escape route for tax evasion.

The false presentation of "internationalism" as a benign influence by the discredited parties of both left and right, for their different reason, has long since been exposed as an imposture on the credulity and goodwill of the majority. As argued in an earlier chapter, an international nationalism should be encouraged, in creating a stable and peaceful world of mutual understanding. It may also be noted that despite the record of history, in planning for the future, nationalism need never be seen as threatening or hostile to others. Its prime necessity for the future should be seen as a defensive wall against internal financial interests that would strip the country of its rightful assets.

Whilst the above describes essential conditions in gathering the support of the nations and peoples of the world for the leadership of the proposed Tripartite Alliance in the cause of reversing climate change and reducing population growth, etc., we must now again return to the question of the differences between the three blocs, and how possible problems may be alleviated.

As we have already noted, the differences are both political and cultural. Most obvious are the signs of a rift between America and China. Their forms of government and international outlook differ widely. America's unhappiness with her economic relationship with China is slowly moving towards a Cold War situation, and this is exacerbated by China's naval manoeuvres in the Pacific area around the Philippines. The development of a Cold War between these two giants would be a disaster for world peace in an age when understanding and cooperation between peoples has never been greater. It would spell an end to the hope of effectively addressing environmental issues, and even more, the need for population reduction.

America's relationship with Europe is also not a happy one. She is irritated by what she rightly feels is the failure of certain European countries – most notably Germany – in contributing their fair share towards the cost of defence. For over a decade America has been reducing her forces in various trouble spots throughout the world, and this policy has been unchanged with the move from Democrat to Republican administrations. The political mindset of American governments and her people have not only been influenced by cost. There is a general tendency in returning to a state of isolation, exhausted as she has been by the futility and failures of so many of her initiatives.

With the threat of civil conflict in so many parts of the developing world, and particularly in the Middle East, it is time when the *adult* must bring the *child* to order. There are no better terms in which the true situation may be described. The past century has amply demonstrated that it is too often the little countries which are the incendiaries breaking the peace of our planet in igniting conflicts that involve us all. The time has therefore arrived for the advanced industrial economies, irrespective of their political traditions, to unite in asserting their morally greater authority in the cause of peace, the environment, and population control. But how can this be successfully achieved in view of the possible factors that divide them?

It is necessary to promote a set of ideas that transcend the political ideologies of nation states, and most apt in fulfilling such a role would be a contemporary interpretation of the Enlightenment values of the 18th century. The appreciation of Reason and the practicality of the material world, and even the 18th century attitude (or deism) towards religion, would fit in neatly with Confucianism as it has evolved in the modern era. The Enlightenment values that first developed in England and France, as a reaction against 200 years of religious bloodshed, was the greatest civilising influence to have ever occurred in the West, and should remain an inspiration for the future.

In turning to America with its current emotional and reason-destroying religiosity, her people should be reminded of their founding fathers who were steeped in the Enlightenment and rational deism. It was these values that successfully guided America towards freedom, growth and prosperity for many decades. If America is to remain true to her creative origins and national character, she should once again promote the Enlightenment of the past. This is not to diminish the value of religion and the need for churches in every nation state. Priests and pastors should be respected and obeyed, but religion and belief in God should be based on rational or demonstrable principles, and not on mysticism or metaphysical arguments.

Religion should satisfy the heart, but only after it has passed the critical examination of the mind, and the Bible should be given a poetic or allegorical interpretation. Leading Anglican theologians have anyway argued along these lines since the end of the 19th century. John Locke,[7] the most admired and greatest philosopher in contributing to American political thought and the sanctity of property, should also be read for his revealing explanation of the meaning of Christianity.[8]

The Enlightenment values of the proposed Tripartite Alliance may be contrasted with the ignorance, superstition, and destructive religiosity that dominates much of the world today. In the 18th century, the word *Enthusiasm* was a popular pejorative term describing the excess of "feeling" of those who had "caught the religious bug." In his *Dictionary*, Dr. Johnson defined the word as, "a vain belief of private revelation, a vain confidence of divine favour or communication." In an age of

---

[7] See John Locke's *The Reasonableness of Christianity, as Delivered in the Scriptures* (1695).
[8] Those interested in the topic of deism and rational religion should consult my book, *Deism and Social Ethics*, that updates the topic for the 21st century.

rationality, following 200 years of religious conflict, religion was respected, but only after "enthusiasm" had been cleansed from the mind. It was a century when more volumes of sermons had been published than in any other, but such churchmen were more intent on interpreting Christianity from a secular moral perspective than in considering the abstruse complexities of religious doctrine. They were practical men of learning, writing with elegance, whilst keeping mysticism at bay.

The peoples of the three blocs we have identified, irrespective of individual status, nonetheless share in this collective superiority over those who do not as yet belong to the advanced industrial economies. But over time, as we have stated, all peoples will be included in an egalitarian world, where no nation state may be judged as any better or worse than another.

In addition to promoting the cultural ideals of the Enlightenment, other practical measures are required in bringing the peoples of the leading countries into a closer relationship. This would be achieved through establishing international friendship associations based on occupations, student circles, sporting or leisure pursuits, or other interest groups. Bona fide marriage bureaux may also be founded in strengthening international connections. All these countries would contribute in disseminating knowledge, and greater understanding and concord throughout the globe.

A unifying comradeship and love, in the realisation of their higher status as civilised beings, should be promoted amongst the peoples of the Tripartite Alliance – irrespective of the nation state. This book is dedicated to the example of the Finnish people in the personal knowledge they are amongst the best governed in the world – although this is not to suggest they are any better governed than the other four Scandinavian states. The point to be made is that all countries within the Alliance have much to learn from each other, and that size plays no part in assessing the quality of governmental systems.

In turning to nation states worldwide, all should seek to promote their own best interests as they decide, and their first priority should be self-sufficiency through maximising home-based productivity as we have already argued in an earlier chapter. All nation states should exert absolute authority within their domain in resisting external pressures, apart from those exceptions concerning the environment or population control, as described in this book. The need for appreciating the wide diversity of political systems and cultures necessitates the above.

It may be that there exist political, social, or legal conditions, in some countries that shock or even horrify those living in others, but it is not the business of one country to interfere with that of another. Such horrors are sometimes never brought to see the light of day – or are never widely publicised – probably because they are countries with whom others have long and successful trading relationships they are reluctant to upset and on whom they are dependent for essential supplies. In the world of diplomacy, silence is sometimes the better part of discretion. Although discreet diplomatic approaches may be made from one country to another, or petitions raised, the rights of a nation state should protect it from external interference when these are a threat to harmonious relationships.

In accordance with safeguarding cultural integrity, every country should define what either constitutes or conflicts with such characteristics. Furthermore, in defending cultural integrity and in warding off the risks of degeneracy, each country should have the right to identify those residents who by their number are judged as undesirable, and hence may be marked for deportation. Such residents would usually be illegal immigrants, but they might be others, or even passport holders of the country concerned. In the latter case, their acquired nationality, or right of residence, may be withdrawn, and together with others categorised as contrary to the public interest, may be deported to the countries of their birth, or other nation states through agreeable arrangements that may be made. Such deportations would be made through compensation payments to deportees, or through prior agreements for employment in the receiving territories.

The above proposals would give acknowledgement to developing countries globally that their relationship with the Tripartite Alliance in no way underestimated their value or unique status as independent countries, and so their right to protect their cultural integrity through effective means. It should be borne in mind that the primary cause for the degeneracy of cultures and civilisations stems from the immigration of those who never can nor wish to be integrated into another society. Rome is an ever-present reminder of a civilisation so destroyed.

In regard to population reduction policies, this should equally apply to the peoples of the three blocs as it would to developing countries Every country would have a target reduction population policy, and this is set out in an Appendix.[9] The difference between the population policies of the countries of the Tripartite Alliance and others, is that in the first, deportation would only affect immigrants and those judged resisting integration; whilst in the second, any might be selected for deportation on grounds of population excess alone. This is explained by the fact that in the countries of the Tripartite Alliance in the northern hemisphere (and Australia and New Zealand), all ethnic peoples have a falling birth rate that needs to be reversed; whilst in the developing countries of

---

[9] See page 123.

the southern hemisphere, there are almost everywhere excess populations that call for reduction.

This returns us to the question as to how far authority may go in pursuing population polices. Where are the limits to be drawn? Is it possible to define such limits? The best we can do in preparation for such policies is to search for, and seek to implement the highest ethical standards in regard to every aspect of political life. In practical terms this primarily means the maximising of justice as fairness, and freedom of thought and action for the total population of nation states, or humankind in general. This book has been an honest attempt to lay down and present such principles, but the limitations of its attempt are recognised. In such a task, the conscience may be cleansed, and the soul purified, in easing the way for a broader sphere of action.

Irrespective of decisions taken, they must be free of guilt or sense of wrong. Let us recapitulate the situation: it is a question of saving the environment, and not only all human, but all animal life – and even flora, from extinction. And the problem is self-inflicted through two causes: firstly, through the complex development of technological civilisation in bringing greater material comforts to humankind; and secondly, through accidental and unforeseen circumstances in triggering a population explosion that cannot be halted, and is exacerbating an environmental catastrophe that cannot be reversed and will inevitably destroy life on the planet. The situation is reminiscent of *The Sorcerer's Apprentice*, as related in Goethe's poem, *Der Zauberlehrling*. As we humans initiated the crisis, only we can resolve it.

There are two ways in which we may respond: either through a fatalistic or accepting pessimism, that argues that this is God's punishment for our sins on earth, and hence the Day of Judgement is nigh; or else, a positive and hopeful optimism, that drives us towards a practical solution in reversing a doomsday scenario. Both alternatives may be supported by their differing ethical arguments. If the first is supported, there will doubtless be a worldwide religious revival, and our churches will be filled, and priests, pastors, and enthusiasts of all religions, will raise their arms in gratitude and joy at God's merciful beneficence with the promise of eternal life in the thereafter. This, of course, has been the traditional and natural human response to major disasters for thousands of years until recent times.

The second or modern alternative is dictated by Reason, Knowledge, and determination to better our future as earth-bound beings in the face of any threats whatsoever. Reason and Innovation reject the idea of the "impossible" as both defeatist and immoral. The modern man or woman would even go further by arguing that belief in the un-demonstrable or fantastic, for whatever reason, is not merely duplicitous and immoral but obscene to an extreme degree. This is because those who preach such "inspired" ideas are the "privileged chosen" exploiting the gullibility of the innocent and uninformed.

If a rational or deistic interpretation is given to the meaning of God, it may be argued it is a God-given duty of humankind to search for and implement any practical means in resolving our environmental and population problems, even if acts of extremism are called for consideration. In this book we have considered socio-political issues in the broadest Social Ethical context. But social ethics differs from Personal Ethics, in that the latter is concerned with the overall thoughts and actions of the lone individual in matters of right and wrong. Social ethics, on the other hand, is concerned with the collectivity of society, usually through the political decision-making of governments, and although such decision-making may often cast a shadow on the total population of a country, and may in some way reflect on the recurring characteristics of many individuals in a nation state, it is not the same as Personal ethics.

The revelation of personal ethics is a far more difficult matter, not only because the confession of the individual may conceal truth, or fail to interpret all wrongs for what they are, but because the subconscious plays tricks on the mind in preventing any real revelation of a person's moral status. We have cited examples in earlier chapters of this book where a sense of guilt is groundless by any objective consideration of the surrounding circumstances, and where such guilt leads to wrong-thinking and social ills in society that should never arise. Even the existence of such a thing as free will is open to question. All that a person may do is rely on his conscience, and when called-upon to carry out an act of extremism in testing his feeling of doubt, all he may do in preparation is to undergo a ritual cleansing or act of religious purification.

Thus, when a 14th century Christian Knight feels morally obliged to carry out a justified act of extremity in the Swedish legend of The Virgin Spring, as portrayed in Ingmar Bergman's prize-winning film, *Jungfrukällan* (1960), he (Max von Sydow) undergoes a ritual cleansing and self-flagellation with birch twigs, before carrying out the deed. Also, in the real world at the present time, on a certain day of the week, there are countries where a dozen or so men undergo ritual purification in the name of their religion, before leaving the house of God in snow-white robes into a square packed with thousands before fulfilling their act of extremity.

Such deeds are only called into being in situations of extremity, and the causes for such are many and cannot be predicted or defined in advance. The problems with which we are now confronted, and have been discussed in this book, remain unresolved and the answer remains uncertain. It is only to be hoped that the final solution stems from decisions that are planned and deliberate. This is because the alternative, i.e., the unanticipated spontaneous outbreak of violence and chaos from no particular or intentional direction, would be the worst possible outcome. Such an occurrence would mean the suspension of ethical purpose through the failure of ability or willpower to resolve the situation through conscious means. Therefore, in confronting the problem, a resolution for action should be thought through and decided upon, and then implemented with moral courage, even if extreme measures are considered necessary.

The ethical question that now confronts us is unparalleled in the entire history of humankind, and is beyond the experience or thinking for consideration by any religious body of knowledge up until the present time. All three Abrahamic religions have traditionally placed the welfare of humankind not only as the focal point for ethical conduct, but until very recent times, that all earthly things should serve his benefit by right. Over the past century, in response to the rape of the environment resulting from industrialisation, mainstream religious thought has moved ahead more towards a Buddhistic approach in recognising the sanctity of all animal life, and further, that the inanimate physical world also calls for acknowledgement and respect.

There is no religious thought to my knowledge, however, that goes so far as to call for the sacrifice of human life in the environmental cause of sparing the planet and all non-human animal and plant life from extinction. And that is the ethical question that faces us today. Will religious thought adapt yet again in adopting such a course, or must it remain as an ethical issue solely within the secular sphere?

If the main theme of this book is the question of population control and reduction, there may be many readers who consider the greater part of its content as irrelevant to the issue, but that is not the case. We cannot act with decisiveness unless our conscience and ethical convictions are clear, and this necessitates the secular intellectual purification of our political mind on all major issues towards that end. This can only be achieved through an objective understanding of those background questions contributing to the maximisation of justice as fairness, freedom, and practical governmental democracy for all humankind, and determination to bring this about.

Only through such a perspective of existence can the highest possible social ethical standards be achieved. That is why it has been necessary to discuss in some depth the hard practical facts surrounding the financial-industrial institutions, the barriers to free thought, democracy, and society in its differing aspects. Perhaps the chapter on political censorship is the highpoint of the book, since it most clearly exposes the corruption, dishonesty, and rottenness of the existing establishment. Here we find a group of authoritative and reputable journalists of a famous publication, who are slapped down for seeking out and expressing the factual truth.

In regard to the discussion on democracy, we have shown how the left/right divide has developed evil consequences in exploiting selfish or subjective motives, that compound rather than resolve problems, in trivialising the latter or addressing them superficially. That is why it is necessary to achieve firm ethical convictions, through sound knowledge and good judgement, so that we have the moral strength to pursue those policies thought essential.

If the conclusion of this book is seemingly incomplete, it is perhaps the problem rather than the author who is at fault.

ADVANCING TECHNOLOGICAL CIVILISATION

There are some things to which there cannot or should not be given a final answer. It is probable that the population question has been pushed further forward in these pages than ever before – but that is not necessarily in itself sufficient. The author and those who have followed this discussion with sympathy, would welcome an alternative or better set of proposals – but only if they bravely confront the hard facts endangering our existence. All else would be a pretentious waste of meaningless sentiment. What matters most of all is the uninterrupted advance of our Technological Civilisation as the first priority of humankind.

APPENDIX

World Population Figures for 2020

The proposed population reduction figures for all countries cited below have been calculated according to differing criteria that may be prioritised within the following categories:-

1. Need for reduction of total world population figure;
2. Need for population reduction in country cited;
3. Maximising the comfort zone of the particular territory;
4. Consideration of the existing population density;
5. Special demographic factors increasing population difficulties, as desertification, or water shortages, etc.; &,
6. Chronic warlike conditions that would benefit through population reduction.

The countries are listed in the following order:- 1. Within the advanced *Technological Civilisation* or the proposed *Tripartite Alliance* comprising, a) Europe; b) North America (including Canada) with the addition of Australia and New Zealand; and, c) The Confucian countries of China, South Korea, Japan, Taiwan, Hong Kong and Singapore; and 2. Fifty other most populated countries elsewhere in the world. All countries are listed in order with the highest population downwards.

APPENDIX

a) EUROPE

Country	Population	Per km density	Proposed Reduction figures
Germany	83,783,9442	240	7,000,000
Britain	67,886,011	281	17,000,000
France	65,273,511	119	10,000,000
Italy	60,461,826	206	14,000,000
Spain	46,754,778	94	6,000,000
Poland	36,846,611	124	5,000,000
Romania	19,237,691	84	3,000,000
Netherlands	17,134,872	508	7,000,000
Belgium	11.589,623	383	5,000,000
Czechia	10,708,981	139	2,000,000
Greece	10,423,054	81	2,000,000
Portugal	10,196,709	111	3,000,000
Sweden	10,099,265	25	2,000,000
Hungary	9,660,351	107	2,000,000
Austria	9,006,398	109	3,000,000
Serbia	8,737,371	100	1,000,000
Switzerland	8,654,622	219	1,500,000
Bulgaria	6,948,445	64	500,000
Denmark	5,792,202	137	700,000
Finland	5,540,720	18	100,000
Slovakia	5,459,642	114	200,000
Norway	5,421,241	15	100,000
Eire	4,105,267	72	50,000

APPENDIX

Country	Population	Per Km density	Proposed Reduction figures
Croatia	4,105,267	73	50,000
Albania	2,877,797	105	70,000
Lithuania	2,722,289	43	700,000[10]
Slovenia	2,178,938	103	50,000
Latvia	2,886,198	30	700,000
Estonia	1,326,535	31	700,000
Luxembourg	625,978	242	50,000
Malta	441,543	1,380	60,000
Iceland	341,243	3	1,000
Liechtenstein	38,128	238	1,000
Gibraltar	33,691	3,369	5,000

Grand total:- 85,637,000

b) NORTH AMERICA, AUSTRALIA & NEW ZEALAND

U.S.A.	331,002,651	36	25.000.000
Canada	37,742,154	4	7,000,000
Australia	25,499,884	3	5,000,000
New Zealand	4,822,233	18	500,000

Grand total:- 37.500.000

---

[10] The high population reduction figures for the 3 Baltic states of Estonia, Latvia and Lithuania, are accountable to the return of their Russian populations through a friendly arrangement with the Russian Federation. These Russian minorities are unable to enjoy full benefits in these foreign territories, e.g., in regard to higher education, and hence their return to their homeland would benefit their cultural future and happiness.

APPENDIX

c) THE CONFUCIAN COUNTRIES

Country	Population	Per Km Density	Proposed Reduction figures
China	1,439,323,776	153	50,000,000
Japan	126,476,461	347	10,000,000
South Korea	51,269,185	527	2,000,000
Taiwan	23,816,775	673	1,000,000
Hong Kong	7,496,981	7,140	500,000
Singapore	5,850,342	8,358	100,000

Grand total:- 63,600,000

-2-
50 OTHER MOST POPULATED COUNTRIES

India[11]	1,380,004,385	464	200,000,000
Indonesia	273,523,615	151	50,000.000
Pakistan	220,892,340	287	70,000,000
Brazil	212,559,417	25	80,000,000
Nigeria	206,139,589	226	90,000,000
Bangladesh	164,689,383	1,265	100,000,000
Mexico	128,932,753	66	60,000,000
Ethiopia	114,963,588	115	70,000,000
Philippines	109,581,078	368	40,000,000
Egypt	102,334,440	103	40,000,000
Vietnam	97,338,579	314	50,000,000
Democratic Republic of the Congo	89,561,403	40	50,000,000
Turkey	84,339,067	110	20,000,000

---

[11] It must be conceded that Indian governments in the past have made serious measures in the attempt to control population growth, but all without success.

APPENDIX

Country	Population	Per Km Density	Proposed Reduction figures
Iran	83,992,949	52	15,000,000
Thailand	69,799,978	137	10,000,000
Tanzania	59,734,218	67	10,000,000
South Africa	59,308,690	49	15,000,000
Myanmar	54,409,800	83	15,000,000
Kenya	53,791,296	94	10,000,000
Colombia	50,882,891	46	7,000,000
Uganda	45,741,007	229	5,000,000
Argentina	45,195,774	17	5,000,000
Algeria	43,851,044	18	6,000,000
Sudan	43,849,260	25	8,000,000
Iraq	40,222,493	93	8,000,000
Afghanistan	38,928,346	60	7,000,000
Morocco	36,910,560	83	7,000,000
Saudi Arabia	34,813,871	16	6,000,000
Uzbekistan	33,469,203	79	7,000,000
Peru	32,971,854	26	6,000,000
Angola	32,816,272	26	6,000,000
Malaysia	32,255,435	99	6,000,000
Ghana	31,072,940	137	10,000,000
Yemen	29,825,964	56	8,000,000
Nepal	29,136,808	203	8,000,000
Venezuela	28,435,940	32	8,000,000
Madagascar	27,691,018	48	6,000,000
Cameroon	26,545,863	56	6,000,000
Côte d'Ivoire	26,378,274	83	6,000,000
Niger	24,206,644	19	4,000,000
Sri Lanka	21,413,249	341	6,000,000
Burkina Faso	20,903,273	76	6,000,000
Mali	20,250,833	17	6,000,000

APPENDIX

Country	Population	Per Km Density	Proposed Reduction figures
Chile	19,116,201	26	3,000,000
Kazakhstan	18,776,707	7	2,000,000
Zambia	18,383,955	25	5,000,000
Gautemala	17,915,568	167	4,000.000
Ecuador	17,643,054	71	3,000,000

Grand total:- 1,179,000,000
Grand total of all 4 categories:- 1,364,207,000

Guide to Further Reading

The following books not only set out to present a practical programme for the future, but more significantly, to create a new thinking or approach to political life for a just and upwardly aspiring egalitarian society. Perhaps more important still, they repudiate what has now become the self-destructiveness of the left/right divide. All the books cited below are addressed to the enquiring general reader, no less than to the academic or specialist –

The Crisis of Democracy *in the advanced industrial economies*
ISBN 978-1-911593-30-0 pp. 130 Demy 8vo, Index

Problems confronting the financial-industrial system, or the ills of the casino economy, have never been more urgent than they are today. This is because debt has reached unprecedented levels in threatening the future of us all, and leading commentators have concluded that it is not a question of *if* but *when* the next banking crash occurs.

Financial issues are compounded by the fact that the left/right conflict through which democracy has long resolved political issues is now failing as a medium in advancing progress. This has more easily allowed raw financial power to neuter democracy and take over party systems across the political spectrum.

Meanwhile, a new middle majority is emerging in displacing the middle and working classes that once predominated in society, and this has led to the collapse of old-established party memberships and voting figures. A positive outcome of these social changes is a more open society that is not prepared to tolerate the secret world of the great corporations, or to accept the word of their politicians in allaying fears for the future.

This book presents a critique of both Neoliberalism or so-called "privatisation" or unconstrained free market forces, and left-leaning ideas on the management of business. In repudiating the principles of both left and right, the author, who is broadly experienced in the spheres of both industry and politics, calls for a new approach in building an economy that is fair and successful in creating a dynamic business culture.

This is to be achieved through prioritising commercially viable productivity over the pull of rentier or usurious tendencies that limit output. These principles, based on the empirical evidence of our toughest industrial competitors in the Post-War period, are designed to unify the socio-economic interests of the emerging 90% majority. The *phony* economy has had its day for too long. Now is the time to promote the *real* economy.

Emergence of The New Majority, being Volume I of
Social Capitalism in Theory and Practice
ISBN 978-0-9556055-3-6   pp. xxxv/282   Royal Octavo
Notes, Appendices, Bibliography, Index

After analysing what should be the remit of political discussion in the *real* world, in differentiating between utopian and practical politics, the author describes the mismatch between the outdated mind-set of political parties and the transformation of society and the world of work over the past 60 years. This has increasingly led to the compounding rather than the resolution of major political problems. The breakdown of the old middle and working classes and their values is traced historically, and it is shown that this was brought about through changing patterns of employment, legislation towards a more egalitarian society, and other economic factors.

The emergence of the new middle-middle majority, with its different values, occurred whilst the political establishment was hardly aware of the fact. Although this new class is highly heterogeneous, at the same time, its specific but unheeded economic needs will eventually act as a catalyst for change. As a new class consciousness emerges through the realisation of these needs, the middle-middle majority will mutate into the all-powerful Responsible Society. The book concludes by addressing several current issues as an exercise in applying Social Capitalist principles.

The People's Capitalism, being Volume II of *Social Capitalism in Theory and Practice*
ISBN 978-0-9556055-4-3   pp. xx/461   Royal Octavo
Notes, Appendices, Bibliography, Index

This book begins by examining the nature of power in the contemporary world: in the world of politics, and more significantly, in the financial-industrial sectors which dominates the first. It examines how power is exerted in the Third world, and compares this with power in the advanced industrial economies. The limits of democracy and federations in upholding the interests of majorities is pointed out, and there is a call for radical changes to the economic system. Part II is concerned with socialising Productive capitalism and how this may be achieved politically. Part III entails an in-depth analysis of Rentier and Productive capitalism: how they operate internationally, and comparisons of their benefits and dis-benefits to society, and their differing macro-economic influences.

Part IV presents a pro-active strategy for the industrial trades unions in working to transform their employing enterprises from the Rentier to the Productive model. Part V on the Human Priorities of Politics delves into a number of philosophical and moral topics on society and government: e.g., on expediency versus justice; the self-justifying cynicism of vested interests; political realism in the just society; how to maximise the individual's potential; and, the desirable foundations for a disinterested politics. The book concludes with a description of the Responsible Society.

Prosperity in a Stable World, being Volume III of *Social Capitalism in Theory and Practice*
ISBN 978-0-9556055-5-0   pp. xx/473   Royal Octavo
Notes, Appendices, Bibliography, Indices

The book opens with 7 chapters on redefining the benefits of free trade in a world dominated by Productive capitalist economies. In such a world legislation would be in place to ensure that international trade was equitable and non-exploitative. There would be an end to usurious lending or investments, and instead, structures would be put in place for releasing the dead capital of the poor through extra-legal arrangements. The new practices of free trade would be linked into meeting the needs of the environment.

Part II is concerned with strategies for national prosperity, and describes the essential basics for a just economy in very simple terms. Such concepts as productivity, wealth creation, and ownership as a stewardship, are given precise definitions. Government policies for industry, and new modes for funding enterprises are covered in detail. Part III is concerned with job creation for Social Wealth. It begins by differentiating between Social and Unsocial Wealth Creation, and describes how industry and jobs have been undermined by Rentier capitalistic practices. Towards correcting the imbalance between public and private sectors, occupational priorities are listed according to productivity; the invisible barriers to trade are identified; and proposals are put forward for reversing manufacturing decline, together with special legislation in increasing the profitability of the productive sector.

Part IV on reforming the business enterprise is concerned with the nature of the Company: identifying its intrinsic purpose; fairness and efficiency as one; and a proposed General Purposes clause for the company. There is also a chapter which discusses the different concepts of usury and as to their relevance today. Part V: Forty-Three Failing Britain, an exercise in the critique of Rentier capitalism, is an attack on a powerful group of corporate directors following their letter published in *The Times* shortly before a general election. Part VI concludes the book with a 49-page Declaration of Social Capitalist Values.

Egalitarianism of The Free Society *and the end of class conflict*
ISBN 978-0-9556055-2-9   pp. xviii/317   Royal Octavo
Notes, Bibliography, Index

This book is an adjunct to *Social Capitalism in Theory and Practice*, in that it expands on several subordinate yet important themes raised in the 3-volume work. Part I comprises 6 chapters on the relationship between Culture and Egalitarianism. Then follow 11 chapters on the Politics of Property which examine the psychological nature of possession, and in pursuing the argument of one of the greatest 19th century philosophers, the author demonstrates that the individual can only reach his full potential through the ownership and use of property.

Property is then described in the different forms in which it occurs in society, including communal and collective property. Part III, Democracy: Real and Illusory, begins by outlining the erosion of freedom in the contemporary world, followed by a clear differentiation between the democratic way of life and democratic government, and how the one may exist without the other. For example, whilst India purports to have a democratic government, its society is severely wanting in democratic values. Singapore, on the other hand, has an ideally democratic and multi-racial society, but its government tends towards authoritarianism. Several commonly held beliefs about British democracy are exploded, and there is a discussion as to when the benefits of democracy are maximised.

The book concludes with 12 chapters on the Road to Constructive Politics, being a critique of 20th century epistemological theories and practices, acting as a barrier to constructive thought. In the revolt against reason, philosophical pragmatism is targeted for particular criticism. The nature of reason is examined, and the reality of ideas is upheld as an essential tool for the intelligent discussion of the material world. The book concludes with an appeal for establishing a New Idealism, the proponents of which would use a methodology very different from their predecessors.

The Future of Politics *with the demise of the left/right confrontational system*
ISBN 978-1-906791-46-9   pp. xvi/188   Demy 8vo
Notes, Index

The left/right confrontational system is coming to an end, since it is failing to further promote the interests of majorities

GUIDE TO FURTHER READING

worldwide. For 200 years it has acted as the linchpin of democracy, and politics is almost unthinkable without referring to the concepts of the Left or the Right.

This book describes how the old confrontational system has fulfilled a vital function for the progress of humanity, but how in advanced industrial economies everywhere, it is now reaching the end of its useful purpose. This is not only reflected in the collapse of party memberships globally, but in the tendency of legislation and the executive to compound rather than resolve the issues of our age.

Meanwhile, a new class is emerging in the advanced industrial world, which the author describes as the middle-middle 90%+ majority. Because contemporary parties are trapped in a time-warp of the past, they are unable to represent the interests of this new majority.

The most urgent political issue of our time – heightened by the debt-fuelled financial crisis – is the need to make the banking and corporate sectors socially responsible. This book outlines a practical strategy towards this end. Only when that is achieved will it be possible to address effectively such pressing issues as climate change.

Over the past 60 years society and the world of work have been transformed out of all recognition. Whilst the world of actuality has raced ahead, political thought has lagged behind – unable to keep apace with the significance of real events.

In the light of this situation, the author points to the necessity for a fresh approach to political thought in breaking the existing mould. New and more effective democratic mechanisms are needed to ensure a socially just and equitable society for a better future. Hence the now malign left/right concepts of the past must be repudiated forever.

The Democratic Imperative *the reality of Power Relationships in the Nation State*
ISBN 978-1-909421-14-1   pp. viii/234   Royal Octavo
Notes, Index

Democracy understood as people power, which is the only proper definition of the word, is put forward in this book as the panacea for resolving the most pressing issues of our time. But democracy as a practicable system hinges on many conditions which are seldom appreciated by our world leaders, international institutions, or relevant bodies of learning.

The evolution of democracy as a system of government and way of life, and the problems to which the former gives rise is broadly discussed by the author. Of most significance are those situations, in both East and West, when democracy is ideologically used as a cover for ulterior purposes.

It is powerfully argued that the left/right divide which for 200 years has served as the rationale for advancing social progress in sustaining democracy is now *destroying* it, as partly witnessed through the collapse of both party memberships and voting figures in most advanced industrial economies. This has occurred through the transformation of society and the world of work over the past 60 years, and has left our parliamentary representatives trapped in a time-warp of the past in their inability to meet the actuality of contemporary issues.

It is clearly shown, through a variety of reasons, that democracy as an all-inclusive system of government is only workable within the nation state. This partly explains the crises of the EU, and the shortcomings of the UN's Security Council. The greatest threat to democracy, since it limits the power of the nation state to carry through electoral promises, is international finance and transnational corporations, which are unaccountable to any responsible authority and liable to bring economic catastrophe in their wake.

This is a book which seeks to empower our national politicians, irrespective of party, so they may more effectively represent the interests of their electorates. A way must be found for our politicians to resolve their predicament, even though it may entail a shift in their attitudes and ideals.

The Death of Socialism *the irrelevance of the traditional left and the call for a progressive politics of universal humanity*
ISBN 978-1-906791-14-2   pp. xvi/174   Demy 8vo
Notes, Index

The author wrote this book after 14 years as an activist, both locally and nationally as a Labour party member. He describes his efforts to update the thinking and attitudes of the party to fit the needs of today's contemporary majority. With this in mind, he attempted to establish a New Socialism, which would not only be more objective in outlook but eschew class-based prejudices. The purpose of politics in the 21st century, surely, was not to nurture old resentments or fight old battles, but to resolve substantive issues in creating a just and egalitarian society.

Although Labour party members today rarely openly promote the idea of class struggle, the author discerned a deeply-felt psychological attitude which was more concerned with "knocking" the opposition than resolving difficult issues for the benefit of all society. Worse still, the attitudes and actions of the Labour party and socialism betray they are not fighting for a classless all-inclusive society, but rather for a proletarian society modelled after their own ideals in discriminating against the rest of the population. The final chapters of the book argue it is necessary to transcend the self-destructive conflicts of the past, through practical politics ensuring an all-inclusive society for justice and equity for all.

Populism Against Progress *and the collapse of aspirational values*
ISBN 978-0-9543161-8-1   pp. xviii/152   Demy 8vo
Notes, Index

This book opens with a description of the hidden poison of populism which is not only undermining democracy but threatens to destroy Western civilisation. In the second chapter this is contrasted with the beneficent power of culture with its channels for creativity on one hand, and bonding mechanisms for understanding and communication on the other. There then follow chapters on the populism of Islamic fundamentalism and how this is hindering the progress of their own people; the battle for freedom through education; social bonding through cultural education; and how populism is adversely affecting the achievement of an upwardly aspiring egalitarian society.

This leads to considering the self-destructiveness of contemporary politics, followed by chapters on corporate power and the corruption of society, and the debasement of culture through marketing strategies. The book concludes with a consideration of those philosophical and educational influences which may be called upon to combat populism and promote higher aspirational values.

Deism and Social Ethics *the role of religion in the third millennium*
ISBN 978-0-9543161-9-8   pp. xx/201   Demy 8vo
Notes, Appendix, Bibliography, Index

GUIDE TO FURTHER READING

Following a period earlier in the 20th century when it was assumed that secularism had finally come to dominate political life worldwide, in the 21st century we now find ourselves living in a very different environment. The influence of religion in political life is now becoming increasingly significant in many parts of the world. In those areas where majorities are more intellectually developed, i.e., in Western Europe and the Confucian countries of the Far East, secularism remains firm in politically guiding the future.

Two questions are raised in this book: firstly, it has now been physiologically demonstrated that the religious temperament is an essential part of the human psyche (although differing in intensity from one person to another) and hence it is ineradicable. The issue in the modern world, therefore, arises as to the desirability of religion without superstition or revelation. The second question arises as how best to communicate with those regimes dominated by religion when the latter is the only basis for personal trust. The author argues for integrity and truth in considering religious questions, as otherwise insincerity and falsehood may lead to mistrust and the failure of political negotiations in the international sphere.

The book presents the need for the deistic beliefs of the early 18th century, but updated with regard to defining the nature of the deity. It promotes a form of deism, based on reason and philosophical principles, enabling a first step on the ladder of religion without commitment to myth, superstition or theology.

Deism as an approach to religion would therefore ideally fulfil the healthy sceptical needs and love of freedom, of enlightened humankind in the third millennium. Meanwhile, in the realm of diplomacy, in acknowledging with conviction the existence of God, it would help bring different faiths towards a common political purpose. The book also presents a critical review and appreciation of leading faiths throughout the world.

Freedom From America *for safeguarding democracy and the economic and cultural integrity of peoples*
ISBN 978-0-9543161-5-0   pp. xviii/222   Demy 8vo
Notes, Appendices, Index
  Also available in Arabic, published by Dar-Al-Salam in Cairo
www.dar-alsalam.com

The book opens with the contention that "the American mindset is distinct from that of any other people or race on earth in a way that no other peoples or races are distinct from one another." Whilst acknowledging that America has produced valued bodies of specialised learning and research, and assenting with G.K. Chesterton's quip, that "the real American is all right; it is only the ideal American who is all wrong," the author then begins to analyse these false values which have made the American character. These stem from a particular type of materialism, whereby money and its acquisition is put on a pedestal above human and other values. This has led inevitably not only to an extreme form of greed, but to deceit and the disguising of motives and attitudes in the service of material gain. These unpleasant characteristics are in turn covered up by a false amiability and superficiality in human relationships.

Out of such a society has developed a highly sophisticated Rentier capitalistic system offering a wide range of usurious financial products. The opening chapter describes an international situation whereby America finds herself versus the rest of the world, in terms of corporate power, and a political ideology convinced it has a God-given mission to culturally absorb all peoples throughout the planet. Chapter 2 is concerned with America and the Deception of the World; Chapter 3 is entitled America and the Debasement of Cultural Values; and Chapter 4, America and the Debasement of Democratic Values, through the emergence of the plutocratic state.

The last two chapters discuss ways in which the world may be liberated from American hegemony. Chapter 5 is entitled, A Global Strategy for the Planet and Humankind, in considering environmental issues in addition to an enlightened business culture, and the need to confront America as an ethical imperative. The last chapter, De-Fusing the Causes of Terror, investigates the injustice and anarchy in many parts of the world stemming directly from American intervention, either direct or covert through such agencies as the CIA. World terrorism can never be defeated through the American war machine – although it may be worsened. It can only be defeated through enabling justice and granting national rights to oppressed peoples.

Our Swindling Finance Houses *their exploitation of the vulnerable*
ISBN 978-0-9538460-5-4   pp. xxi/121   Demy 8vo

Using the pseudonym of Guy Tallice, the author describes his horrific 6-month stint in working for a major finance services company, and household name, at the end of the 1980s. Having been made redundant as a senior executive of a manufacturing enterprise, and desperate to find work to keep up mortgage payments, and maintain a family with 3 young children, he joined Allied Dunbar as a Sales Associate.

The book opens with a Preface sub-headed Swindling Within The Law, which examines in some detail different modes of fraud and sleight of hand used to confuse or deceive the public. He shows how financial services use swindling methods throughout the industry, and concludes with an appeal for legislation to define and make swindling an illegal activity. He then vividly describes the guile of recruitment methods, and the ingenuity of deceit in inveigling the unemployed into their organisation.

During the Thatcherite era when industries were going bust and unemployment was soaring, there were only Phony Jobs in A Phony World, being the title of the opening chapter. The second chapter, Ripe for Exploitation, describes in detail the pain of unemployment together with its adverse psychological effect on the personality, and the stress it brings to family life. The third chapter, What Dreams are Made of, describes the recruiting procedures, with promises of riches for those working for the company. The fourth chapter, The Glory Days, outlines the author's working experience and early success.

Using hard-selling methods, after an intensive training course, he approached every relative, friend, neighbour, and casual acquaintance, to buy Personal Pension plans. In addition, he approached industrial enterprises, and in one factory sold personal pension plans to a number of semi-literate manual workers on the minimum legal wage. Back at the office he was held up by the branch manager as an example of the ideal Sales Associate. The author, however, could meanwhile not understand the downcast attitude and apparent apathy of colleagues – or not until it was too late.

The subsequent chapters expose the huge swindle inflicted on Sales Associates, each of whom supposedly had a separate and secret arrangement with his manager on the mode of remuneration. The author called a meeting of his colleagues and they cooperated in a rescue plan for disengagement from the company, meeting secretly in the office late in the evening, and using available facilities in photocopying CVs in an attempt to find real jobs. Although the author was never paid the commission he had earned, and incurred heavy debts by the time he left the company, he escaped lightly by comparison with several colleagues who lost their homes and personal assets, due to extortionate loans forced on them by managers to maintain business and living costs.

When the swindle was finally uncovered, the author turned on his colleagues, asking why they had not warned him of the fraud into which they had all fallen. Their simple answer was: "But we all had our different arrangements and we didn't know what yours were. When the mask was taken off we just felt stupid. Now don't you feel the same?" – "No," replied the author, "I just feel swindled." Drawing together all the facts, he wrote to Sir Mark Weinberg, Chairman of the company who had been knighted the previous year at the instigation of Margaret Thatcher for developing the financial services industry. The letter was copied to several other directors. The letters went unacknowledged, but the matter was passed to senior managers who called a meeting to talk through the problem, but despite flattering gestures, discussions ended in futile circular arguments.

The author's career with Allied Dunbar was brought to a sudden halt following serious injuries during a crash as a front seat car passenger, after signing up a major contract with an engineering company, together with a senior colleague, as they sped away at high speed in elated spirits, realising they would shortly be £4,000 richer. After 3 years litigation, the author was persuaded (through the burden of debts) to accept a derisory compensation payment from the company for his injuries. Shortly after hospitalisation, the author visited his remaining colleagues in their office to be cheerfully met with the revelation that Allied Dunbar had arranged for them to receive

Social Security benefits. And these were the employees of one of the wealthiest financial services institutions in the UK!

The final chapter proposes reforms in cleaning up the industry. In the first print run of the book there was, absurdly, a Dedicatory Petition to the Labour Government elected into power on 7th June 2001, to "initiate legislation to curb the greed dishonesty and scams of the financial institutions." It was not fully realised at the time that the Labour government would promote the interests to the usurious economy to Thatcherite proportions.

Land of The Olympians papers from the enlightened Far North
ISBN 978-1-906791-17-7   pp. 264   Royal Octavo
Notes, Index

This book reprints articles originally published in the 1960s in the Finnish press and learned journals, during the author's 10-year residence in Scandinavia. The leading series of 8 articles, *How To Be An Olympian*, were published in the country's leading intellectual journal, and comprise a study of neutrality in Sweden and Finland and how it affected social and political attitudes. The author praises the cool objectivity and sagacity of neutral Scandinavians in their socio-political outlook, comparing this favourably with the stressful, excitable, and often prejudicial environment of those countries unhappily caught up in the Russo-American conflict.

Here was a haven of peace, security, and sanity, in a world which was otherwise constantly in fear of nuclear war. The author raises the question of Britain and Continental Europe forming into a neutral but militarily powerful bloc, possibly at the instigation of Gaullist France, as a defence against the ideological fanaticism of Russo-America. Two other series of articles, published in Finland's second largest daily, comprise studies of the entrenched English class system, comparing it with the egalitarian and democratic societies of Scandinavia, with their higher living standards and greater freedom.

Other articles (several of which were illustrated with cartoons) take a wryly humorous look at Finnish life; and then there is a short story, *What The Watchdog Saw*, being a savage satire on the skulduggery of both the left and right in the Britain of the 1960s. The book concludes with a lecture, *Internationalism and Europe*, originally delivered in 1964, in which the author argues that Europe is ideally placed, through her greater maturity, to take realistic measures for establishing a more peaceful world in intervening between the abrasive political extremism of two larger powers.

The Social Capitalist Network
www.socialcapitalistnetwork.org

INDEX

A

Academics, devaluation of 78 et seq
Afforestation 25
Africa 40, 46, 47, 103
Albert, Michel (1930-2015) 57, 89
America, 9, 20, 21, 23, 39, 41, 47, 50, 51, 57, 69, 103, 110, 111, 112
Antarctica 89, 99
Anthropocene extinction 104
Anti-business ethos 59
Arabs 30
Arctic 70, 99,
Asia 30
Asimov, Isaac (1920-92) 101
Attenborough, David 15, 16, 101
Augustus Caesar (63 BC-14 AD) 43
Australia 12, 18, 31, 39, 115

B

Bangladesh 46
Bank Directors 54
Barber, Lionel 92, 94
Barclay brothers (David & Frederick) 71
Beaverbrook, Lord (1879-1964) 71
Bible 112
Birth rates 29 et seq, 43
Black Death (1346-51) 27

Blair, Tony 66, 86
Bradbrook, Gail 101
Brazil 32
Brexit 19
Britain 17, 21, 47
British Economic Crisis, The 90
British press 71 et seq
British stock exchange 55
Broadcasting entertainment 73 et seq
Brown, Gordon 86
Burke, Edmund (1729-97) 62
Bursting at the Seams (2007) 100

C

California 69
Campaign for Industry 90 et seq
Canada 12, 18
Capitalisme contre Capitalisme (1991) 58, 89
Carrington, J.C. 89
Catholics 29
Cato the Elder (234-149 BC) 44
Censorship 85 et seq
Charles, Prince of Wales 102
Churchill, Sir Winston (1874-1965) 83
Chekhov, Anton (1860-1904) 73
China 9, 12, 18, 20, 21, 22, 23, 29, 49, 50, 57, 103, 110

INDEX

Chomsky, Noam 81
Civilisations 16 et seq, how they emerge 36 et seq, vulnerability of 43, et seq
Civil servants 87
Clark, Kenneth (1903-83) 45 46
Class in politics 62
Climate change 9, 25
Cold War 9, 56, 110
Coleridge, S.T. (1772-1834) 77
Colonialism 35, 38
Columbus, Christopher (1451-1506) 17, 22
Confucian cultures 12, 18, 21
Congo, Dem. Rep. of 103
Constructive thinking 11, 69 et seq, 80 wt seq
Cooperative Bank 90
Cousteau, Jacques (1910-97) 101
Covid-19 27
Craig, W.L. 82
Cultural integrity 114

D

Dasgupta, Sir Partha 101
Deism 111 et seq
Democracy 9, 21, 23, 49, 59 et seq
Denmark 20
De Qincey, Thomas (1785-1859) 76
Desalination 25
Difference & equality 38
Diversity principle 47, 48, 68, 75
Drug culture 76

Dual-party confrontation 23

E

East India Company 39
Easter island 28
Edwards, George T. 89, 90
Egalitarianism 66 et seq, 78
Egypt 44, 103
Ehrlich, Anne 100
Ehrlich, Paul R, 26, 100
Ellis. Havelock (1859-1939) 43
Emerson, R.W.(1803-82) 9
English language, devaluation of 77, 78
Enlai, Zhou (1898-1976) 50
Enlightenment values 111 et Seq
"Enthusiasm" 112
Environment 9, 25, 96 et seq, response to catastrophe 116 et seq
Equality 61
Essay on the Principle of Population, An (1798) 26
Estonia 20, 125 fn
Ethics, social & personal 117, 118
Ethiopia 103
EU 19, 20
Europe 12
Explaining New Ethics for Survival (1972) 100
Extinction Rebellion 101

F

Financial-industrial system 49,

INDEX

50 et seq, 88, 106 et seq
Financial Times 91 et seq
Financing Industrial Development (1979) 89
Finland 113
Far East Tiger 52, 56, 57
France 31, 40, 57
Frazer, Sir James (1854-1941) 36
Freedom, conditions for 70 et seq
Free market 58
Freedman, Milton (1912-2006) 52

G
Gandhi, Mahatma (1869-1948) 52
Germany 56, 57, 87, 110
Ghettoization 47
Glaciers, retreat of 98
Goodall, Jane 101, 102
Gozzard, Dr. A.B. 90
Goethe, J.W., von (1749-1832) 116
Goyder, George (1908-97) 88
Gregson, Lord (1924-2009) 90
Greece 31
Greenland 98
Grylls, Sir W. (1934-2001) 89
Guillabaud, Prof. J. 101
Gulf States 30

H
Hallam, Roger 101
Hammerfest 29
Hampshire, Susan 96, 101

Harden, Garrett 100
Harmsworth, Alfred (1865-1922) 71
Hart, Dr. John 90
Hayes, Adrian 35
Heat-trapping gases 97
Henry VII (1457-1509) 17
Henry VIII (1491-1547) 55
Higher education 11
History of Civilisation (TV Series 1969) 45
Home-based productivity 21
How Economic Growth & Inflation Happen (1984) 89
Hume, David (1711-76) 80
Hunter-gatherers 36
Hyper-inflation 64

I
Ibsen, Henrik (1828-1906) 73
Ice cores 98
Ideology 62
Immigration 31 et seq, 43
Imperialism 41, 42
India 30, 39, 103, 126 fn
Industrial Revolution 55
Inequality of peoples 41
Integration 47, 48
IPBES (Intergovernmental Science-Policy Platform on Biodiversity & Ecosystem Services) 104
Italy 31
IUCN (International Union for Conservation of Nature) 105
Japan 12, 17, 18, 29, 57
Johnson, Dr. Samuel (1709-84)

112
Jungfrukällan (1960) 118

K
Korea 12, 18, 57

L
Labour party 65 et seq, 86
Left/right divide 9, 10, 23 16 et seq
Leverman, Anders 99
Liberal party 86
Lipton, Martin 93
List, Friedrich (1789-1846) 55
Living Planet Report 104
Locke, John (1632-1704) 107, 112
Lovelock, James 26, 69
LSE (London School of Economics) 79

M
Macaulay, T.M. (1800-60) 93
Malta 29
Malthus, Thomas (1766-1834) 26
Marcuse, Herbert (1898-1979) 81
Marxism 81
Maxwell, Robert (1923-91) 71
Mexico 31
Middle East 111
Middle majority 10, 60 et seq
Ming dynasty 22
Moon, Twila 99
Moral values, evolution of 83
Mozart, W.A. (1756-91) 45

Münter, Leidani 29
Murdoch, Rupert 71

N
Naess, Arne (1912-2009) 101
NASA (National Aeronautics & Space Administration) 97, 98
National Farmers' Union 108
National interests 24, 109, 110, 114
Nelson, Horatio (1758-1805) 83
Netherlands 18, 40
New Agenda, The 91 et seq
New Guinea 46
New Zealand 12, 18, 31
Nicholas II (1868-1918) 18, 115
Nigeria 103
Nixon, Richard (1913-94) 50
North Africa 31
Northern hemisphere 29

O
Official Secrets Act (1911) 87
Old middle class 10, 60
Old working class 10, 60
Oregon 69
Osborn, Frederick (1889-1981) 101

P
Packham, Chris 101
Paglia, Camille 82
Pakistan 103
Pandemics 27, 28
Parkin, Sara 26, 50, 101
Personal debt 63
Personalisation of Ownership

INDEX

107 et seq
Personal Pension Plans 64
Philippines 9, 110
Plato (c 428-348 BC) 45
Policy Foresight Programme
  101
Polarisation of society 63 et seq
Political censorship 11, 85
  et seq
Pollard, Prof. Sidney (1925-98)
  90
Population Bomb, The (1968)
  100
Population Explosion, The
  (1990) 100
Population question 11, 16, 25
  et seq, 103 et seq, 115
Postmodernism 11, 81 et seq
Potsdam Institute for Climate
  Impact Research 99
Potts, Malcolm 26
Pragmatism, political 62
Productive capitalism 52 et seq
Productive profitability 108
Protectionism 57
Protestants 29
Poverty 16

R

Racial mixing 47
Radio 4 93
Rainforest 25, 32
Reagan, Ronald (1911-2004) 52
Refugees 31
Reith, John (1889-1971) 73
Religion 112 et seq
Renewable power 10

Rentier capitalism 53 et seq, 68,
  106, 109
Reversing Industrial Decline
  (1981) 89
Rock"Roll 76
*Role of the Banks in Econmic
  Develolpment, The* (1988) 89
Romano-Hellenic civilisation
  39
Rome 17, 38, 43, 44
Revolution of 1905 18
Reykjavik 29
Rockefeller, John D. (1839-
  1937) 101
Rural land ownership 108
Russia 18, 19
Russell, Bertrand (1872-1970)
  101

S

Sach, Jeffrey 101
Sanger, Margaret (1879-1966)
  101
Santa Maria 22
Scandinavia 57
Scruton, Roger (1944-2020) 82
Shakespeare, W. (1564-1616)
  45, 73
Shaw, G.B. (1856-1950) 73
Shriver, Lionel 85
Siberia 70
Singapore 12, 18, 21
Smith, Adam (1723-90) 56
Smith, Keith 90
Socialism 58 et seq
Society, transformation of 23,
  primitive 36, intermediate 39

INDEX

Solar panels 10, 25
South America 30, 59
Southern hemisphere 29
Soviet Union 19, 59
Spain 17, 31
Spanish flu 27
State of Nature Report (2016) 105
Strindberg, A. (1849-1912) 73
Students, their intolerance 82, 83
Study of History, A (1954) 45
Super-rich 64
Sydow, Max von (1929-2020) 118

T
Taiwan 12, 18
Tanzania 103
Technological Civilisation 9, 11, 12, 15 et seq, 20, 24, 31, 33, 35 et seq, 46, 69, 78
Territorial expansion 23
Thomas, Terry B. 90
Thomson, Lord (1894-1976) 71
Thatcher, Margaret (1925-2013) 52, 57, 86
Thunberg, Greta 102
Tickell, Sir Crispin 26, 59, 100
Tidal power 25
Today programme 93
Tory party 86
Toynbee, Arnold (1889-1975) 44
Tragedy of the Commons (1968) 100
Tripartite Alliance 12, 18, 20, 21, 23, 24, 33, 48, 103, 113, 115
Turkey 31

U
Unity Trust Bank 90
United Nations 33, 103, 105
UN Millennium Project 100
Usury 58

V
Virgin Spring, The (1960) 118
Vladivostok 29

W
Walters, Alan (1926-2009) 52
Wars of the Roses (1455-1485) 17
Washington (State) 69
Wealth polarisation 44, 58
Wilhelm II (1859-1941) 18
William, Duke of Cambridge 102
Wind-power 10, 25
Wolf, Martin 92, 94
WWF (World Wildlife Fund) 104

X
Xiaoping, Deng (1904-1997) 50

Y
Yakutia 70
Youth Culture 75 et seq

Z
Zedong, Mao (1893-1976) 50

www.ingramcontent.com/pod-product-compliance
Lightning Source LLC
Chambersburg PA
CBHW020805160426
43192CB00006B/445